ISELIN

The Rich History of a Western Pennsylvania Coal Town in Appalachia

The Inspiring Story of Unrelenting Citizen Advocates for Social Justice

Sara Lambert Bloom

ISBN: 979-8-218-95177-1

Printed in the United States of America by 48HrBooks

Front Cover:

Rolling Hills of Appalachia, photo taken by Stan Semuskie

Power House, Tipple, and Pig's Ear, 1904, vintage photo

Groundbreaking for the Sewage Demonstration Project and Presentation of a plaque to Sara, the widow of James P. Lambert, surrounded by 2 of their 5 children and 6 of their 15 grandchildren, photos taken by a Lambert family friend.

Back Cover:

Alex Semuskie painted by Billy Perry

Dedication

To all those who resided in Iselin, Pennsylvania over the last 120 years
since its founding in 1903: I hope and pray that I did justice to your story.

And to their unrelenting citizen advocate for social justice, Mr. Jim:
Thank you for your voice, your good heart, your belief in what can be,
and your hard work to bring relief to Iselin.
You were what we all would be.

—In celebration of my hometown & my family's good life there.

Kind regards
Sara
July 2023

Acknowledgments

Thank you to all the wonderful people of Iselin who trusted me with their memories and their deeply personal stories. They are named in the Notes section of the book. In the Epilogue are even more of their anecdotes and information they generously provided that I was unable to fit into the main body of the book.

Their authentic voices are the soul of this story.

I want to extend heartfelt gratitude to Michael Duffalo and Stan Semuskie along with all the others who contributed vintage photographs that vivify the story of Iselin: Alex Semuskie, Debra Askins Semuskie, Andrea Jean Ploskunak Hallman, Ruth Durand Shields, Mary Menotti Abbati, the Lambert family, the booklets printed by Holy Cross Church to mark their Golden and Diamond Jubilees, DownEast Magazine, and Dr. Harrison Wick, Associate Professor, Special Collections Librarian and University Archivist, Indiana University of Pennsylvania (IUP) Libraries.

Thank you to Abby N. Wells for her support and interest in this story.

And a special thank you goes to Alex Semuskie, third generation coal miner and Iselin's talented and devoted historian and collector extraordinaire of mining artifacts.

Prologue

"The history of coal mining goes back thousands of years, with early mines documented in ancient China, the Roman Empire, and other early historical economies."

Table of Contents

Chapter 1

Passing Forward the Inspiration

If we are to make progress addressing the social justice issues of the coal industry or indeed of any industry, the successes of unpaid citizen advocates to eliminate life-threatening health hazards and inhumane hardships using both local, state, and federal grants and the courts need to be told and retold, inspiring current and future generations of citizen advocates to step up and earn the badge of being "unrelenting" in seeking ways to hold owners to an acceptable standard of compassionate treatment of workers and their families and to an acceptable standard of environmental quality.

Chapter 2

The Need for Coal

> Along with the change to factory production, there was a basic shift in the source of energy, from human to steam. The Industrial Revolution was ultimately driven by steam-engines fueled by coal. As it progressed [1880-1930] so did the demand for a plentiful and *cheap* source of coal energy. In America that source was bituminous coal, found in the Appalachian Mountains which run from Pennsylvania to northern Alabama. *National Park Services: Appalachian Cultural Resources Workshop Papers* (1880-1930).

After the first phase of waterpower, generated by a fairly benign invention of putting a water wheel or turbine into a forceful stream of water or a waterfall, the Industrial Revolution in America was ultimately driven by steam engines fueled by burning coal. This introduced both unacceptable levels of pollution of the environment and unacceptable levels of dangers associated with coal mining. There is little that could be called benign about the working conditions endured to extract coal from underground mines in this second phase of America's Industrial Revolution or about the harsh living conditions that powerful coal companies imposed upon the miners and their families.

This book tells the story of that human drama, the rich history of a Western Pennsylvania coal town in Appalachia that arose at the nexus of industrial development in America and its voracious appetite for cheap power, while narrating and celebrating the inspiring story of successes achieved by unrelenting unpaid citizen advocates for social justice.

Chapter 3

My Mission As an Author and My Growth As a Person

Even beyond that, as I came to write this book some 78 years after having been born in Indiana [PA] County's General Hospital that Adrian Iselin, Jr "presented" to us coal people in 1914 and having been raised in Iselin along with my four siblings, it struck me just what it meant that, along with many other Pennsylvania coal towns, our town was owned. I want readers to give this some thought; it played a huge role in our drama. We were owned.

> Our jobs, our houses, our water, our heat source, our sanitation, our air quality, our medical services, our churches, our cemetery, our schools, our company store, our post office, our polling station, our hotel, our theater, our sports teams, all owned. If we had had a bank or a gas station, they too would have been owned. Competitive retail stores were kept out of town. With owning comes total control.

We were first owned by the owner of a coal company that founded our town in 1903 and then 44 years later the entire town was bought by the owner of a salvage company. The stark differences between the two experiences are revealing.

I want students, our future policymakers and unpaid citizen advocates for social justice, to discuss in their classrooms whether residents in America are still owned, albeit not by a single entity as we were, living on a variation of a Southern plantation and trying to make ends meet in an economy that has been described as feudal.

But that said, the deeper I "mined" the story of my heritage, the more I realized what a rich pocket of humanity I grew up in. A deep vein, as they say in coal company parlance. And the more I realized what could and could not be owned. I came to appreciate the spirit and loving habit of our embracing each other's joys and sorrows and our sacred traditions of coming together to mourn our losses. I admire in hindsight our resilience and transcendence as a community, much of it expressed in our music and art and poetry and in our academic and athletic prowess, in our high spirits and good humor, and in our capacity for hard work. We felt blessed to live in a structured society that valued our schools and churches, our sports, and yes, the law enforcement that kept order in the town. And we held firm to our belief in social justice and held firm to our belief in our self-worth, leading us to believe that we deserved better working and living conditions and leading us to believe that we should expect better.

How many can describe their hometowns of any size in those terms? From birth I sensed that I belonged, that my family and neighbors lived in a way that spoke to what we all held dear—each other.

Chapter 4

The Beginnings of Iselin

The Pittsburgh Gas & Coal Company, a subsidiary corporation formed by officers of the Rochester & Pittsburgh Coal & Iron Co. (called R&P) purchased a 105-acre farm along with its big farmhouse, which affectionately became known as "the Big House," from Julia Ann Rosborough on February 25, 1903, land on which to build housing for workers they would recruit from Europe to mine a recently discovered vein of bituminous coal. Ms Rosborough, the 14th child of James Rosborough and Mary Deemer Rosborough, was born in 1844 in nearby Elders Ridge, a small village that had its beginning in 1786, where a rich vein was already being mined in 1903.

Located a little over one mile northwest of the proposed new coal town, residents of Elders Ridge distinguished themselves in the 1830s by founding the Elders Ridge Presbyterian Church to serve residents who were primarily farming families before coal mining was established there. This led to the founding of the private Elders Ridge Academy where the Church's pastor taught, beginning with an enrollment of 31 pupils in 1847. Lucius Waterman Robinson, R&P's Chief Executive from 1899 to 1919, gave the Academy $3000 to float the institution when it ran into financial difficulty in 1910. The Academy later went through several transitions, becoming the Elders Ridge Vocational School in 1914, a pioneer school of its type in the state, ultimately becoming a public school in 1937 serving grades 7-12. Due to mergers, the school buildings are now abandoned, not yet torn down. Ridge View Cemetery, established a century earlier, was incorporated in 1908 and remains lovingly kept by its Board of Directors, but the community has recently had to tear down the 1830 Elders Ridge Presbyterian Church after it fell into serious disrepair.

The concept of establishing employment, housing, church, cemetery, and school was the prevailing norm then, remaining to this day a successful formula for business entrepreneurs. But what took Elders Ridge over a century to develop was about to happen in a scant few years a mile away.

Patch towns were small towns established near already established coal towns, built to house the miners closer to a newly discovered vein. In September 1903 the small community being created was named Iselin in honor of Adrian Georg Iselin (1818-1905), the New York banker, owner of several railroads, chief investor in the Rochester & Pittsburgh Coal and Iron Co, known as R&P, and financier. Eminently successful, his firm was so strong that it helped to finance the United States Government at the outbreak of the Civil War.

Going back further into the family's history, Adrian Georg's father, Isaac Iselin (1783-1841) was born in Basel, Switzerland where, according to Wikipedia, the Iselin family had been wealthy merchants, public officials, military, and professional men since the 14th century. Isaac and his wife Aimee Jeanne (née Roulet) Iselin emigrated to America from Switzerland in 1801, building on the fortune that the Iselin family had amassed in Switzerland, working from their new home and offices in New York City. Adrian Georg, the fifth of eleven children born to Isaac and Aimee in NYC, learned from his father the work of importing and banking, investing in railroads, and creating mining companies and coal towns and coke ovens. Isaac also schooled Adrian Georg in the art of philanthropy.

One of Adrian Georg's sons, Adrian Jr (1846-1935), was the eldest of seven children born to Adrian Georg and Eleanora (née O'Donnell) Iselin (1821–1897); Eleanora was a member of a prominent and wealthy Baltimore family.

Upon Adrian Georg's passing, Adrian Jr, a second generation Swiss-American, along with one of his brothers, inherited the management of their father's investments and companies including the town of Iselin, a new coal town in Indiana County that had been named in Adrian Georg's honor when it was created in 1903, just two years before his passing. The Iselins must have had high expectations for Iselin, Pennsylvania; other coal towns that they built bear the first names of their children.

R&P's Chief Executive Lucius Waterman Robinson was charged with recruiting the workers. In a letter he wrote in 1902 to Mr A.J. Davis, an Agent at the Reading Terminal in Philadelphia, Mr Robinson responded to a proposal made by Mr Davis's brother "to establish an agency in Philadelphia for the employment of labor to work at [your] mines." Mr Robinson anticipated needing approximately 1000 workers for the new mines R&P planned to open over the next year or two. He wrote, “We are willing to pay their fares, if necessary to get the men, the amount of fare to be deducted from their wages when they get to work. Of course, we would want him to get as many to pay their own fares as possible, as they would be more apt to stay. We have good shanties which we rent from $2.00 up to $5.00 per month, and good houses which rent for from $5.00 to $6.00, and which are plastered, painted, and have good cellars. The men will have no difficulty in getting good shanties or houses to live in, or good boarding with people of their own nationality.”

In this letter Mr Robinson specified in no uncertain terms the ethnicity of the workers R&P would employ, details of which are discussed in Chapter 12 of this book.

First to arrive in Iselin in 1903 were the workers, about 400 men at first, swelling in number to 675 by 1904, who built the railroad tracks out from the pits to transport the mined coal; they also built the Coal Tipple, Power House, and Train Station and laid the foundations for the mine drafts and for the town's planned housing/outhouses.

From the start, electric motors were installed inside the mines to haul coal out and up into the Tipple, an innovation that reduced the number of animals used underground. The maternal uncles of my father, James P. Lambert, were coal miners around the town of Grampion, near DuBois, PA, in the early part of the 20th century. “Horses were used to pull rail cars in funiculars and coal mines as early as the early 16th century. The earliest recorded example is the Reisszug, Austria inclined railway dating to 1515. Almost all the mines built in 16th and 17th century used horse-drawn railways as their only mode of transport." In Grampion, PA in the early 1900s, they used donkeys. According to my late brother, James M. Lambert, "Will and Ned Gribbin worked regular shifts mining coal and they were also given the job of exercising, feeding, and watering the donkeys that were used to haul the wagons loaded with coal out of the mines. This was considered 'overtime' for Ned and Will, but the mine boss was not able to pay them in cash as that would complicate his tax situation. So Will and Ned agreed to take payment of real estate for their compensation. And that's how the family came to own the farm on South Main Street in Punxsutawney. The 1920 Federal Census shows the house 'owned, free of mortgage' by Will Gribbin. And the 1924 City Directory for Punxy [as it was known locally] lists Will Gribbin as Superintendent of the Elk Run Coal Company, and living at the farm at South Main Street."

So those electric motors in the Iselin mines were not only efficient but also proved to be a huge cost savings for R&P.

An entrepreneurial baker set up a huge outdoor oven near the huts and tents of those first workers, supplying more than 1,000 loaves a day of fresh-baked bread. "Living conditions were difficult at best; bathing and other matters of personal hygiene were difficult to accomplish. Cold, wet weather made life in the tents miserable, with frozen toes and fingers becoming simply a normal part of life."

By early 1904 a true town had begun to form. Many of these men stayed on to become the first miners to be hired, having arrived alone from Poland and Italy as well as from Czechoslovakia, Slovakia, Hungary, a few from England, and later from Ukraine, those being married eventually bringing over their families and most others finding brides after they were settled, joined by a small group of local native American Indians, as they were called, who were taught to mine. The first housing for the miners continued for a time to be the group of tar paper shacks built down by the newly erected Power House and Coal Tipple; they called this shanty town the Pig's Ear.

Following other books that have explored more of the mechanics and the bossing of the challenging work of underground bituminous coal mining, this book brings to life the effects on the miners and on their families of that hard and dangerous work through the weaving of historical documents, vintage photographs, and spoken anecdotes into the researched narrative—all of which I found fascinating. One small detail that I just learned, for example, is the critical but less hazardous work of the Iselin Gandy Dancers who kept the train tracks leading from the mines to the tipple swept of lumps of coal that inadvertently spilled onto the tracks in transit. The term "gandy dancer" is allegedly a combination of the name of Chicago-based Gandy Manufacturing Company, a maker of track-lining tools, and the description of the workers' dancelike movements.

This book tells a story with many layers, the telling of which invites the reader to imagine how his or her life might have been in Iselin.

Complex levels of danger and hardship, complex layers of pure joy and happiness along with sadness and grief are described within these pages, all experienced in the pursuit of extracting coal-black lumps of industrial power from the unforgiving depths of the earth.

FIG. 3. POWER HOUSE AND TIPPLE, ISELIN PLANT

Power House, Tipple, and Pig's Ear, 1904

Opening to Iselin Mine No 2, 1903

Boiler Front and Jones Stokers, Iselin Plant

Iselin Gandy Dancers-train track laborers

Miner without helmet undercutting coal seam

July 11, 1902.

Mr. A. J. Davis, Agt.,
727 Reading Terminal,
Philadelphia, Pa.

Dear Sir:-

Your brother proposes to go to work for us with a view of establishing an agency in Philadelphia for the employment of labor to work at our mines, which he will send on from time to time. I write you, as I do not recall his initials, and you can refer this letter to him.

We want mainly good Italians, Polanders and Hungarians. We do not want any colored help, or Irish, under any circumstances, nor do we want any hard coal strikers. We would like to get green labor mostly, or such as have been in this country but a short time, as they will soon work into the work we have to offer. We can use a large number of men for loading coal in the mines, cleaning roads, mining coal with machines, which they soon learn, as outside labor on our tipples dumping coal, and also on our coke ovens in connection with loading coke, drawing coke, and for common day labor. I would propose when he gets a bunch of men together, if they are Italians, to send an Italian interpreter who works here in the mines to tell them that we have no strikes or labor difficulties, and who can assure them that they can get good work and wages in this region. If the bunch happens to be

R&P letter 1902, p.1

Mr. Davis, -2-

Polanders or Hungarians, I can send one of that nationality to assist your brother and convince them that they are to go to a favorable place to work.

We are willing to pay their fares, if necessary to get the men, the amount of fare to be deducted from their wages when they get to work. Of course, we would want him to get as many to pay their own fares as possible, as they would be more apt to stay. We have good shanties which we rent from $2.00 up to $5.00 per month, and good houses which rent for from $5.00 to $6.00, and which are plastered, painted, and have good cellars. The men will have no difficulty in getting good shanties or houses to live in, or good boarding with people of their own nationality. For common labor we pay $1.50 per day. Coke drawers make $2.55 per day, and coke loaders $1.60 per day. The machine miners get 38 cents per ton, and dumpers on tipples anywhere from $1.50 to $1.75 per day.

We can use some of these men at our mines at Yatesboro, the junction station with the B.R.& P. being Echo. We can also use some at Du Bois, Reynoldsville and Punxsutawney. We expect to open several new mines this Fall, which will give employment to a good deal of common labor, as well as miners, so that we can use this Fall probably 1000 men placed around at our different mines which will absorb this number. Tell your brother that he will have to keep in touch with us, writing often and reporting progress, and where I do not want to do any advertising, I want him to work it himself and get together what men he can around the docks and other places. We do not care for any English-speaking

R&P letter 1902, p.2

Mr. Davis, -3-

labor being sent here, for it is too apt to be strikers and cast-off labor from other mines.

Very truly yours,

General Manager.

Chapter 5

The Churches

The miners lost no time in requesting that a visiting priest be sent out to Iselin weekly to serve their needs. Making the 17-mile trip by horse and wagon from St Bernard of Clairvaux Church in Indiana, PA, a parish belonging at the time to the Pittsburgh Diocese, a priest said the first Mass in one of the shacks in the Pig's Ear after the Catholic men of Iselin and the few women already living there worked together to clean it up.

Then in 1905, Mr Robinson, R&P's CEO, wrote to St Bernard's indicating that the R&P Coal & Iron Company was willing to help the people of Iselin erect a church, which they did, naming it Holy Cross Church. This generosity was perhaps a gesture to the founder's family that adhered to the Roman Catholic faith as well as a response to the needs of the workers, although it is reported that Adrian Iselin Jr himself was not a member of the Catholic Church. No longer a mission, its first financial report submitted to the chancery as a parish was written by Holy Cross Church in September 1908.

During the early part of 1918, both the Holy Cross Church itself and the rectory that had subsequently been built in 1912 were destroyed by fire. Undaunted, parishioners arranged for Mass to be said in Iselin's original town hall; several months later, permission to rebuild was granted by the Bishop, along with a gift of $13,000 from the Diocese to help cover costs. In the late 1940s, the final mortgage of $4500 on the church was cancelled by R&P. In 1951, Holy Cross Church became a parish in the Greensburg Diocese.

Holy Cross Church became a focal point for this vibrant community. Daily Mass and two Sunday Masses were said by a resident priest with, during one period, a junior organist paid to play and sing (alone) the Gregorian Mass in Latin seven days a week. These services were well attended, mostly by the mothers, wives, and widows of coal miners. A senior organist played for the second of the two Sunday Masses joined by an adult choir that she directed, having taught them to sing the Gregorian Mass in Latin, occasionally interspersed with hymns sung in Polish. The Catholic men of Iselin typically attended this Sunday Mass along with the women and children. The organ was upgraded over the years, after the organists started out playing a “pump organ” that literally fell apart. The boys were taught the rituals to serve as altar boys, dressed in the full regalia of the Catholic Church; incense was used by the priest during his blessing, creating an ethereal ambiance enhanced by the ornate altar, baptismal font, confessional, elaborate iconic statues to honor Mary and Joseph, the Crucifix, and the plaques that represented the Stations of the Cross that lined the walls. Banners reading Gloria and Alleluia were painted on the ceiling above the altar in celebration of the Resurrection.

"Everyone loved the glorious gladiolas my father grew, admiring them as they walked or drove by our backyard but feeling especially blessed to see the heavenly beauty they brought to the altar and feeling doubly blessed to enjoy the delicate fragrance that filled the Church. Dad delivered large bouquets to Church each Sunday morning when they were in bloom."

Holy Cross Church was a haven, a lifeline to the divine for people who cherished the beauty they found in nature but otherwise were surrounded by the harsh environment of work in and around the mines and the harsh conditions of living in a patch town. For certain serious needs, parishioners came back to Church to pray the rosary together and at times even to pray the Novena (Latin for "nine"), prayers made on nine consecutive days, which Wiki defines as "a ritualistic devotional worship where one or more Christian devotees make petitions, implore favors, or obtain graces by honoring Jesus Christ, Virgin Mary, or the saints of the faith who are believed to empower divine intervention."

Proportional to the size of the Iselin community, Holy Cross Church was a cathedral, having all the majesty minus the presence of an onsite Bishop that qualifies a church to be called a cathedral, but certainly having been blessed by a Bishop's loving care and financial support from the Diocese from its inception in 1908, along with the admirable financial support contributed by the R&P Coal Company for over 40 years.

Throughout most of my adult life I felt angry about the coal company extravagantly spending so much money on the ornate altar and almost nothing on improving our hazardous living conditions. But as I age, I wonder if, given a choice, that wasn't the better choice.

The question is, why not both? And the sad answer is, because it worked for them.

In the 1950s the annual 3-day summer bazaar sponsored by Holy Cross Church became affectionately known as “Big Time,” an outgrowth of the Ice Cream Festival that was started by an ardent parishioner in 1909, her entrepreneurial venture realizing a profit of $25.00. Subsequently it was taken over by the Church after having become “quite a social and prosperous affair” in its very first year, eventually becoming Big Time. But perhaps more importantly, during the long winter evenings there was ping pong and boxing, bingo and all sorts of games to be played in the Church's basement; plays that were performed by the children to the great amusement of all; quilting and needlework groups that gathered to enjoy each other's company and share expertise, producing beautiful pieces for their families and other pieces to be raffled off to benefit the Church; and even a lending library that was set up and well-used by all. Summer entertainment was centered around the popular church-sponsored softball and baseball teams that competed in the county-wide R&P league. While these games thrilled the crowds who gathered to watch, the informal bocce games played by the Italian members of the community were also a big hit. These activities became less and less vital as more and more families owned cars and no longer lived in isolation on the “cultural island” of Iselin.

Through all seasons and all decades, community dinners served in the Church's basement provided occasions for warm and spirited intergenerational social gatherings. As new facilities were added, the ladies of the Church were even able to cook and bake these prized meals there in the basement of Holy Cross Church, featuring ethnic favorites from several cultures.

Early on there was a Church Lodge whose membership numbered nearly 100, mostly men. Later on, adult parishioners of Holy Cross Church connected through membership in the Church-sponsored Holy Name Society for men and the Christian Mothers for women with Senior Sodality and Junior Sodality organizations developing the leadership and inter- and intra-personal skills of the teens and young adults while nurturing their religious grounding. Catechism classes were taught either by the priest or a lay volunteer. "During one period of time," reports one lifetime Iselin resident, "classes [at Iselin Elementary School] ended at noon on Fridays; we went to catechism class at Holy Cross and the Protestants went to class at their Church in Iselin; students who were not members of either Church were kept at School for study hall." First Communion and Confirmation ceremonies were very special occasions prefaced by weeks of religious study required of the children, these classes sometimes being led by visiting seminarians sent out from Greensburg by the Diocese.

"The practice of deducting rent, doctor's fees, church contributions, and store charges from paychecks meant that miners rarely saw cash."

"Even though he was a Catholic coal miner, my father was not happy that $1 was withdrawn from his and the other Iselin miners' paychecks each month to be given to Holy Cross Church."

Holy Cross Church invited my late sister, Jane Lambert Abe to write the "History of the Parish" for the booklet they titled *Golden Jubilee of Holy Cross Catholic Church, Iselin, Pennsylvania 1908-*

1958. This article was published, retitled "Church History" to be included in an article titled "Golden Jubilee Celebration Set Sunday at Iselin Holy Cross Catholic Church," (Indiana, PA: *Indiana Evening Gazette*, June 1958). Her history includes a description of the party held in the early 1940s to celebrate the burning of the $4500 mortgage on Holy Cross Church that had been held by R&P since 1918 and was now officially forgiven.

Jane's narrative is the richest source that I have found of an authentic Iselin "voice" who was there from the very beginning, the woman whom Jane interviewed for the piece, so Jane's article is included in its entirety in #3 in the Epilogue of this book. It is interesting that Jane does not name her, and I regret that I don't know the reason for that, but I find their rapport touching and the details enlightening.

No author is acknowledged in *Diamond Jubilee of Holy Cross Church, Iselin, PA 1908-1983,* a similar but less detailed booklet printed by the Church in 1983, but it does include interesting details of the upgrades made to the Church, paid for by parishioners with no funding contributed by the Diocese. And of course, the Church received no funding from R&P for these upgrades since by then the coal company had sold the town to Kovalchick Real Estate Division in 1947, an entity that did not contribute to this or to any civic improvements in Iselin. The parishioners paid $25,000 to renovate the interior of Holy Cross Church in 1977 and $6000 for the renovation of the exterior in 1978. They contributed the funds needed for the digging of the trenches to support the Church's decision to replace the use of their own well water with "city water" when the new Iselin water tower was dedicated in 1981, and again, parishioners contributed funds needed for the digging of the trenches to support the Church's decision to replace the use of their private septic tank to connect to Iselin's Rural Waste Water plant that was finally in place and available to all residential and civic properties in Iselin in 1982. In 1983 the parishioners donated $6000 to upgrade a storage space and another $6000 to paint the exterior of the Church, indicating the dedication of parishioners to maintain their house of worship, only to be closed by the Diocese just 6 short years later.

But given Iselin's dwindling population, the Greensburg Diocese closed the Holy Cross Church parish in 1989 and after the iconic statuary and elaborate altar were removed, the structure was desanctified and it and the rectory were sold as a private residence. The outdoor grotto honoring the Virgin Mary, built by some of the men of the parish in the early 1940s to enshrine a beautiful outdoor statue of Mary, was actually lifted intact onto a flatbed by Iselin men using a crane and moved in 1989 to the grounds of the Church of the Good Shepherd in nearby Kent, PA. There the parishioners from Iselin's Holy Cross Church joined with parishioners from St Gertrude's Church and St Anthony's Church, two other churches serving the nearby coal towns of McIntyre, Coal Run, and Aultman that were also closed by the Diocese in 1989, to build the new consolidated church that was located in Kent, 7 miles from Iselin. "The new church, parish administration center, and rectory were dedicated in 1992, built at the cost of over $2.2M. The men of the parish physically built the rectory and parish administration center to help defray costs, which significantly saved the parish a large amount of money. The women of the parish would cook meals daily for those working on the rectory project." And the Diocese purchased the land on which it was built, donating it to the new Church of the Good Shepherd. These parishioners bonded, contributing money and labor and were also invited to bring selected pieces of their beloved statuary and stained-glass windows to be installed in the Church of the Good Shepherd. Perhaps most importantly, they shared the history of having been born and raised in a patchwork of diverse immigrant communities with vibrant cultures, languages, customs, and traditions originally established early in the 20th century to mine bituminous coal, held together and sustained by a common factor: a deep and abiding faith.

An admirable undertaking, but it certainly marked the end of the ritual of the widows of Iselin walking to daily Mass. Many had no access to transportation to Kent to attend Sunday Mass.

A cross remains at the top of the steeple of the now secular building that originally was Iselin's Holy Cross Church.

The rectory was purchased by the Hill family who converted part of the two-story home into a classroom and learning center in which they homeschooled their four children in the 1990s, "to work together as a family as well as provide their children with more of a 'life education,'" according to an article titled "Communities in Profile—Iselin, Aultman, McIntytre," written in 1993 by Jeffrey Katarski for the *Tribute-Review*, the second largest daily paper serving metropolitan Pittsburgh, which is located 40 miles southwest of Iselin. A new owner who lives in Iselin has purchased the property and is currently renovating both structures; he plans to rent the two-story former rectory to a new family and convert the former church into an indoor play space for children.

In addition to Holy Cross Church, an inter-denominational Protestant church named Iselin Union Church was built atop the hill just below the town's (only) water tank and adjacent to Iselin Elementary School--just across Cement Road from Holy Cross Church. The two churches were similar in style and dimensions, including their comparable height. The pair made a commanding visual statement overlooking the community, the Company Store having been located down near Lower Street. Due to the large number of Catholics in the town, Holy Cross's parish remained the larger of the two, but the Iselin Union Church established and maintained a positive presence in Iselin.

Few documents have survived, but oral history relates that, like Holy Cross Church, it too was constructed in the 1910s with funding provided by R&P.

Unlike Holy Cross Church, however, Iselin's Union Church continues to function to this day. Known for its inspiring religious services as well as its popular potluck suppers that solidify community bonds, it remains in use by its faithful members.

1908

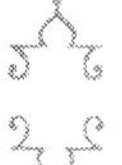

1958

GOLDEN JUBILEE

OF

Holy Cross Catholic Church

ISELIN, PENNSYLVANIA

Iselin Union Church

Inside of the Church Facing the Altar

Church Facing the People

Picture of Church with Rectory

Also Three Day Church Bazaar—

Golden Jubilee Celebration Set Sunday

Interior of Holy Cross Church during a service
Indiana Gazette, 1958

SOLEMN HIGH MASS

OF

THE HOLY CROSS PARISH GOLDEN JUBILEE

Sunday, June 8, 1958, at 12:00 A. M.

PROGRAM

PRESIDING AT MASS .... MOST REVEREND HUGH L. LAMB, D.D.
Bishop of Greensburg, Pa.

CELEBRANT .... REVEREND FRANCIS D. PIRULLI
Pastor of Holy Cross Church, Iselin, Pa.

DEACON OF THE MASS .... REVEREND ALOYSIUS BORKOWSKI
Pastor of St. Mary's Church, Export, Pa.

SUB-DEACON OF THE MASS .... REVEREND GEORGE KILARECKI
Asst. Pastor of St. Mary's Church, New Castle, Pa.

DEACON OF HONOR TO THE BISHOP .... REVEREND V. B. KUKLESKI
Pastor of St. Josaphat's Church, Pittsburgh, Pa.

DEACON OF HONOR TO THE BISHOP .... REVEREND NUNZIO PIRULLI
Pastor of St. Cajetan's Church, Monessen, Pa.

MASTER OF CEREMONIES .... REVEREND NORBERT GAUGHAN
Secretary to Bishop Lamb

SERMON .... THE RT. REV. MONSIGNOR JACOB SHINAR
Secretary to Bishop Deardan

John Lambert .... Cross Bearer
Richard Fello and Robert Fello .... Acolytes
James Gordish .... Thurifer
Michael Condor .... Boat Bearer
James Kaito .... Aspergil

Holy Cross Choir under the direction of Mr. Sam Catalino
Organist, Mrs. Erma Francisco

Organists

Choir

Children of the Parish

Altar Boys

Rev. George Kilarecki

Sister Mary Celeste

Sister Maria Benedict

Sister Maria Goretti

Sr Goretti is Maria Zamberlan

Church Lodge of Years Ago

First Communion Group of Years Ago

Holy Name Society

Christian Mothers

Senior Sodality

Junior Sodality

Top: Holy Cross Softball Boys Team
Bottom: Holy Cross Softball Girls Team

Top: A More Recent First Communion Group
Bottom: May Crowning of This Year

Rochester & Pittsburgh Coal Co.

Indiana, Pennsylvania

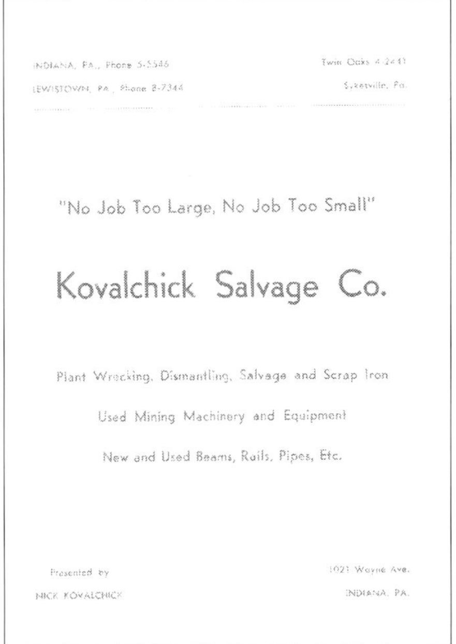

Top Left: R&P Full Page Ad; James P. Lambert along with Frank Caratelli, Stanley Kaminski Jr, & Alfred Kolokowski sold 191 ads for the Golden Jubilee Booklet
Top Right: Lucas Waterman Robinson
Bottom Left: The Second of two Full Page Ads; Kovalchick Real Estate Division also purchased a one eighth page ad.

1908

-

1983

Diamond Jubilee

Of

HOLY CROSS CHURCH
ISELIN, PA

Present sanctuary of Holy Cross Church, c. 1977

Chapter 6

Secular Societies

Iselin's secular societies included the early formation (prior to 1910) of a very popular Italian Band with a fluid membership of 40-50 avid musicians. Hungarian, Polish, Slavish, and Italian lodges and fraternities met regularly in the early decades and an organization called St Peter and Paul's became Branch 400 of the Ukrainian National Association. Meetings of the Ukrainians continued to be held through the mid-1960s in the basement of a home of one of its members, an Iselin coal miner, but sadly ended when they became discouraged that money they were sending to relatives in Ukraine never reached them.

The men always dressed sharply in white shirts, suits, and ties for these lodge and fraternity meetings. For church services and events, the men, women, and children always dressed in their finest, the women always wearing hats in church as is the traditional Roman Catholic custom.

"As children we always had one good outfit that was referred to as our church clothes."

A group of the young men of Iselin relaxing

Iselin Italian Band 1910

Iselin musicians

Ben Braesucker and Andy Ploskunak. Andy was born premature, so tiny that his improvised "incubator" was a shoe box with a hot water bottle. They say that Andy became a very strong man and a fine coal miner, and was always a good looking dresser along with his friend Ben.

Chapter 7

Social Stratification

"In the early days of the town, English-speaking inhabitants held themselves above those speaking foreign languages. This made for an uneasy alliance among Scottish, Irish, American, and Native American laborers. English-speaking workers often became foremen or other management-level employees. Europeans who did not speak English were given more menial positions, which caused dissension in the town. An obvious indicator of the division between cultures was the fact that the goal of many residents of Iselin was a home on English Street, a sign one had 'made it.'"

While this may have been the case in the very earliest days, stratification lasted only until the English language was mastered by the immigrant miners and they too could communicate well enough to be assigned leadership positions.

Social stratification never existed within the Iselin churches and school, the backbone of Iselin society. There was a grace, an effortless bond of mutual respect among residents of Iselin, probably enhanced by shared hardship in Iselin and isolation from the outside world, but this bond definitely was a natural result of being good people with good family and good community values. They did not escape poverty and persecution in their native countries to seek a chance to build anything less than love, respect, interdependence, and communal enjoyment in America.

Beginning later in the 20th century, immigrants often watch TV to learn English. “In the 1920s my father read mystery books and magazines written in English to learn the language. He could recite some of them in English, word for word, from memory.”

While they honored their heritage, it is true, however, that some miners and/or some of their family members altered their names to sound more “American.” And it is reported that attendance at Mass dropped among Italians when Polish priests were assigned to Holy Cross Church, and vice versa when Italian priests were assigned to Iselin by the Diocese. But never was there open dissention among groups. It’s interesting to point out that never was an Irish priest assigned by the Diocese to Holy Cross Church since very few people of Irish ancestry lived in Iselin, a result of the hiring practices of R&P from the very founding of the town.

Chapter 8

The Housing

By 1910 1700 miners were employed in the Iselin mines.

By 1911 approximately 300 housing units had been built, with running water but no indoor tubs, showers, or toilets included in the units. "The picture of the miner's wife scrubbing his back as he squats in a round, galvanized tin tub following a day's labor provides another pervasive image of mining life." This image was immortalized in the 1941 American film "How Green Was My Valley," directed by John Ford and set in Wales.

In Iselin this ritual extended to family members, but for them it was on a weekly schedule. "My mother heated the water [in a big pot on a coal stove] and filled the tub on Saturday evenings, each of us four kids taking turns being scrubbed in the same water for our weekly bath. Being the oldest, I was lucky to be first, getting the clean water. [And from this we learn where the phrase "don't throw the baby out with the bath water" originated!] But we learned early not to complain about anything; after my grandfather was crushed to death in the mines, my father's life as a miner began when he was just 9 years old, picking coal in the pits. My parents were cheerful and loving, bearing their hardships with quiet dignity and doing their best to conceal them from us." They and other families were able to install an electric water heater after having purchased their home in the mid-1960s, making bath time a little easier while still having no installed tub or shower until they could afford the cost, if ever, of the fixtures and installation. The possibility of having an indoor toilet (for those without sufficient land) would not exist for another 20 years.

A woman now in her 90s tells of her and her brother both having been born in an upstairs bedroom of a single house on Lower Street in Iselin. "After the furnace was banked for the night, I remember it being so cold that the insides of our windows were coated with ice. Of course, there was no insulation in any of those houses."

The poet Joyce Rupp writes, "One winter morning I awoke to see magnificent lines of frost stretching across my window panes. They seemed to rise with the sunshine and the bitter cold outside. They looked like little miracles that had been formed in the dark of night. I watched them in sheer amazement and marveled that such beautiful forms could be born during such a winter-cold night." I daresay that no poem has yet been written that captures the emotions felt when waking to see magnificent lines of frost stretching across the inside of one's bedroom window panes, but it wouldn't surprise me to learn that the little girl marveled at their beauty even as she shivered in her bed waiting for one of her parents to go down to stoke the coal furnace.

"I married an Iselin man and when we had a baby, I remember pinning her blankets around her so she wouldn't kick them off in her sleep; I was so afraid her little fingers and toes would suffer frostbite." Her maternal instincts led her to improvise what became known as a sleep sack.

Most of these housing units were built in the design of what was then called "double houses," nowadays called "duplexes" with an outhouse designated for each unit at the end of a pathway; these privies were affectionately described as "two holes and a Sears Roebuck catalog." Each 4-bedroom unit housed 12-14 boarders in the earliest years with miners coming in to occupy beds as other miners went out to work a shift. Meals were served on long wooden tables cobbled together using heavy wooden boards meant to be used for making mine cars. Coal for heating was stored in a coal shed built by the outhouse, the price deducted from the miners' paychecks.

"When my husband was a teenager growing up in Iselin, during the summer months he walked daily down to the boney dump to pick coal, filling a gunny sack which he lugged home up a steep hill. By the time school started in the fall he usually had the family's coal bin filled with free coal for the winter.

"Picking coal" is a term used throughout the book and means just that, whether loose lumps of coal were picked up by children sent into the pits to work or picked up by children scavenging free coal for their families from the boney dump, which is the slag pile where coal that was too low grade for selling was dumped by the coal company.

The electrical grid in the first half of the 20th century in Iselin was typical of the era. "Many different power frequencies were used in the 19th century. Very early isolated AC generating schemes used arbitrary frequencies based on convenience for steam engine, water turbine and electrical generator design. Much later, the use of standard frequencies allowed inter-connection of power grids. It wasn't until after World War II with the advent of affordable electrical consumer goods that more uniform standards were enacted." Oldtimers in Iselin remember the lights in their homes flickering when they used an appliance, before the whole town was converted in 1956 to 60 Hz by V. C. Shields & Sons, a business located in Indiana.

Cover of Coal People, Contemporary Images of Northern Appalachia--Photography by James W. Harris, 1995. Mr. Harris took this iconic photo at the Greenwich, PA mine. It was used by the United Mine Workers Journal for their yearly calendar, becoming known affectionately as "Miss February."

Laying a house foundation in Iselin in 1910. That's an awfully young workforce.

A house being kept up with some paint and the cheerful efforts of a youthful sweeper.

Top: A neglected house but a nice-looking dog.
Bottom: The well-kept Ploskunak home, after they purchased both sides of their double house.

Chapter 9

A Lasting Memorial Sets the Cemetery's Traditions

Brothers Jack and Dominic Ritchey, skilled masons who immigrated very early on from Venice, Italy were responsible for building the foundations of most of the houses and outhouses in Iselin, as well as all the drifts in the mines. They are best remembered, however, for the hand-crafted cement markers made for the Iselin cemetery. Their masterpiece is a remarkable monument that covers the remains of the first man killed in the Iselin mines. The name of the dead man is uncertain due to the ravages of time and vandals, but the eight-foot-high column of cement-covered brick remains. Also gone are the six smaller columns topped by cement urns. An older generation of Iselin residents can remember the grave marker as it originally appeared, complete with realistic miner's cap, carbide lamp, pick and shovel, all carefully modeled in cement by the Ritchey brothers but now replaced by iron replicas. The reconstructed monument serves as a memorial tribute to fatally injured miners in the Iselin Mine 1903-1935, marked by a Tribute held at the Cemetery on Labor Day 2012, titled *Out Of This Mine.*

Dominick specialized in painting ceiling frescoes, and some ceilings in what remains of original Iselin housing still have traces of his paintings.

A Ritchey great-grandson and his wife traveled from Italy in 2021, to spend their honeymoon in and around Iselin, retracing his family's now-legendary legacy in Iselin. They are scheduled to return!

In 1944 a big wooden cross was donated by R&P for the Cemetery.

It is touching that the Iselin Union Cemetery Association is now the focal point of community engagement. Iselin native Clifford Durand, the son of David Durand, an Iselin coal miner, and his wife Josephine, was the manager of the Cemetery from 1960 until his passing in 2004. In more recent times, following the Miners' Memorial tribute that was held on Labor Day in 2012, a Memorial Day Service was held on May 26, 2014, listing in the program the names of 6 Iselin men who are Veterans of World War I, 48 Iselin men who are Veterans of World War II, 11 Iselin men who are Veterans of the Korean War, and 4 Iselin men who are Veterans of the Vietnam War. That list will be kept current by the handful of devoted members of the entirely volunteer Iselin Union Cemetery Association. Among the members are the men who work pro bono to dig new graves, prepare the new headstone beds, and keep up the grounds and the women who also work pro bono to keep the books and organize the events so that funds can be set aside from donations and the sale of plots for creating memorial monuments. These volunteers are the anonymous "Donor" acknowledged on the beautiful Veterans Memorial that they dedicated in a ceremony held on Veterans Day in 2021.

Discussions are being held to decide next how to appropriately honor all those buried in unmarked graves--perhaps as many as 500 who died in Iselin during the "Spanish flu" epidemic of 1918 and others, including some miners, whose burials took place most likely without caskets or funeral services. Donations may be sent to Iselin Union Cemetery Association, PO Box 63, Clarksburg, PA 15725.

Indian graves are located just beyond these unmarked graves; a careful discussion of appropriate preservation efforts/memorial may be next in the Association's continuing dedication to honoring the history of Iselin and its quintessential residents dating back over 120 years.

"I was busy today putting flowers on six graves. We were blessed to have loving families including parents and in-laws, and sure do miss them all."

OUT OF THIS MINE

A MEMORIAL TRIBUTE TO
FATALLY INJURED MINERS IN THE ISELIN MINE
1903 - 1935

LABOR DAY, SEPTEMBER 3, 2012
11:00 A.M.
ISELIN UNION CEMETERY ASSOCIATION
ISELIN, PENNSYLVANIA

OUT OF THIS MINE, A Memorial Tribute to Fatally Injured Miners in the Iselin Mine 1903-1935, Iselin Union Cemetery, 2012

Veterans' Monument close up, Iselin Union Cemetery, dedicated on Veterans Day 2021

Inscription: In Tribute to All Veterans of the United States of America This memorial honors all American Veterans who, although separated by generations, shared a common undeniable goal to valiantly protect our country's freedoms. The memories of these American Veterans and our gratitude will continue to live on whenever and wherever democracy exists. The American Veteran is forever a symbol of heroism, sacrifice, loyalty, and freedom.

"...that this nation, under God, shall have a new birth of freedom and that the government of the people, by the people, for the people, shall not perish from the earth." President Abraham Lincoln, Gettysburg Address

Dedicated By The Donors

Veterans' Monument mounted.

Chapter 10

Living With Conditions in Iselin

Over time individual families occupied the housing. Gardens of flowers and vegetables, grape vines and fruit trees adorned each back yard, Iselin once winning a prize from Indiana County in the 1940s for its horticulture. Picture rows of housing closely spaced on unpaved streets with no sidewalks, housing that had most probably never been painted. Lining the alleyways were rows of ubiquitous outhouses that were pumped out each summer by men affectionately known as "honey dippers," first using buckets fastened to the end of a long pole and later using a big, motorized hose attached to a truck, both systems leaving sloppy, disgusting droppings in the alleys, a known source of disease. The concrete foundations laid under the outhouses in 1904 had begun to crack, allowing constant seepage over the decades. Residents spread lime around the perimeter of their outhouses to keep down the odor, and routinely scrubbed the interiors weekly to maintain some measure of safe hygiene for their families while praying for timely visits from the honey dippers, which did not always happen. Imagine the pall of choking, toxic fumes that hung over the town from the constant burning of the "boney dumps" that surrounded the town, the coal too inferior to sell but highly combustible internally within the piles of slag that were dumped. The women and older children scrubbed the floors of their homes weekly and scrubbed the soot off the interior walls of their homes every Spring.

None of that seemed to dim the spirit of hardworking people who, while relentlessly asking for safer conditions in the mines and in the housing/outhouse stock, loved their families and their flower gardens, their school and churches, and their music and sports, people who bonded with each other and loved calling their children home to supper from the kitchen door. And believe me, you'd come running too if you could smell the delicious aromas coming from those kitchens that were kept impeccably clean!

"I will never forget the sight of a house burning to the ground; there were no firetrucks to come to put out the flames. That happened twice during my early childhood [in the 1930s]. My father had memories from the 1920s that when a miner died at work, his body was brought on a cart pulled by a mule to the edge of the lot where he lived and just left there by the mine crew."

"I'm not sure why the First Aid unit was not called, but one day a miner was brought out of the mine being carried on a door, his back broken. He had no family and was unable ever to work again. My mother took him in, settling him into the wash house adjacent to the Big House until eventually she found it necessary to take him to the Indiana County "Poor House" for better care. I remember us kids cutting down a small Christmas tree and spending hours carefully cracking walnuts along the seam, picking out the meat for Mom’s holiday baking, and gluing the shells oh so carefully back together, with a colorful loop of yarn glued into the top of the shell. How triumphant we felt presenting the injured man, whom we called Shoemaker, with a Christmas tree hung with walnut-shell ornaments and a plate of walnut cookies.”

There were no showers at any of the mine sites until the 1960s, so it was a ritual to greet the stream of miners coming from the Shed built for them on Cement Road where they were picked up and dropped off in Iselin at the start and end of a shift at a neighboring mine, walking from the Shed to their homes where a tub of warm water prepared by their wives or older children awaited them, followed immediately by family supper, continuing the traditional rituals that began when miners had walked home from the Iselin mines covered in black coal dust at the end of a shift beginning a half century earlier.

In 1914, six tons of coal, handloaded, were being brought out of the Iselin mines each day, but over time work ebbed and flowed as the market demand for bituminous coal ebbed and flowed. The miners continued to live with their families in Iselin, “carpooling” to work in neighboring mines after the Iselin mines were closed in 1935, the population of Iselin including women and children having reached as high as 5000 at its peak in the 1930s.

Walnut ornaments recreated in 1985

Iselin First Aid Team practice, 1906

Chapter 11

Civic Developments, Including the Indiana County Hospital and the Iselin Elementary School

An article published by the Indiana Gazette reported on March 3, 1911 "An Epidemic of Fever Down at Iselin - Water the Probably Source of Infection" indicated that the probable source was typhoid.

In response to such serious needs that were beyond the skills of a company doctor who was in residence in each coal town, Indiana County's General Hospital was built in 1914 in Indiana, 17 miles from Iselin, made possible through the philanthropy of Adrian Iselin, Jr in memory of his first wife, Louis Caylus (1848-1909). It became the go-to hospital for treatment for Iselin residents and eventually for birthing, replacing the home birthing commonly used by residents during the earliest years. Still in use, it has been reorganized as the non-profit Indiana County Regional Medical Center, one of the eighteen member hospitals of the Pennsylvania Mountains Healthcare Alliance that was established to provide community-based health care via independent community hospitals.

Typically, just housing and a Company Store/Town Hall were built in a Patch Town but in addition to that stock and their two Churches and a Cemetery, Iselin eventually accumulated a Post Office in the building that housed the Company Store. (An oldtimer remembers that in the 1940s the Post Office was moved from inside the Company Store to a small building with a private entrance that was built attached to the Company Store. That was probably mandated by the federal government as being more secure.) A three-story, 39-room Iselin Hotel (for miners and visiting company officials) was built of wood costing $9000, a small fortune at that time. Also built were the Rex Theater that showed movies 7 days a week in its heyday (1920-ish), a mine office, a small office for the company doctor, and three adjacent school buildings (with running water, except for when the water went dry).

Never a "one-room-school," from the very beginning there were 8 classrooms in the Iselin Elementary School, one for each of the grades 1 through 8 (but no kindergarten), and two 3-seat outhouses, one for girls and one for boys built near the school buildings, the entrance to each concealed by a "blind." By the 1940s most of the 8 classrooms had an upright piano and school days were started with recitation of the Pledge of Allegiance to an American flag that hung near the blackboard and class singing which, beginning in the 1950s, was from books published by the American Book Company titled *Music For Young Americans*. The series was developed by leading music educators (including a professor at Columbia University's Teacher's College, the Supervisor of Evanston IL Public Schools, and others from across the nation). Volume Three, to give an example, includes chapters titled *Starting the Year, We Study*

Rhythms, A Day with the Indians, We Learn to Read Music, February Holidays, We Sing, Play, and Dance, and *From Spring to Summer,* revealing the range of pedagogical aspirations of developers of this series. Towards the Iselin Elementary School's final decades in service, a district music teacher visited periodically bringing a few instruments that were available to loan to pupils who showed interest and aptitude.

"When I was 5 years old, the youngest of 5 children, I pined to go to school with my four older siblings but there was no kindergarten. Often their teachers allowed me to sit all day with my sisters at their desks in their respective classrooms that year. Pure joy."

The curriculum at Iselin Elementary School was very traditional and included lessons in the Patterson method of writing cursive, which seems to be a lost art. "I'll never forget being given specially lined paper and a pen with a metal nib and a bottle of ink. And I can still hear the teacher chanting 'round, round, ready, write' to get us into a rhythmic pattern of writing whatever loops or strokes we were to practice before going on to writing cursive letters or words. I think I wore ink home on those days."

Recess was held twice during the school day as well as a break for lunch, with a variety of ball sports available to play outdoors as well as a swing set, ropes for playing jump rope, chalk for setting up hopscotch, and "running all over the vast grounds playing tag and other children's games." Playing jacks indoors was a big recess favorite of the girls.

A small nearby building was used for periodic visits to the children by a nurse for charting height and weight records and giving eye exams, vaccinations, lice checks, etc. Toothbrushes were given to the children.

"In the 1930s children were given free milk each day at Iselin Elementary School but it was a mystery why one little girl was not being given her carton of milk. Her father finally discovered that when he filled out the required paperwork with the priest, the priest did not approve his application for his daughter to receive the free milk at school, basing the denial on the father being involved in 'making moonshine.' It seems that he was making a small amount of wine in his cellar from grapes he had grown."

The Iselin Elementary School was attended by not only the children of Iselin but also by the children of farming families in the rural area surrounding Iselin and families living in small nearby towns such as Elders Ridge, West Lebanon, and Kent that did not have an elementary school. During the mid-1900s, parents of these students included teachers, a principal, a banker, foundry workers, and farmers. While Iselin children ran home to eat lunch, these children ate their packed lunch at School and often had to walk a mile or so, to and from a centralized bus stop located near their home to catch a ride on the school bus.

"I was one of the few students who rode a bus to school [from Elders Ridge] since the majority of my classmates walked from town. I remember Mrs Baker keeping the big stove going in the winter months. She would put our sandwiches on top of the stove to toast. We felt special but I really enjoyed being able to walk to a friend's house for lunch from time to time. That was a treat."

"I never had a male elementary school teacher" and only unmarried women or married women older than childbearing were hired in that era. The reason for the ban on married women teaching public school seems to have been related to their frequency rate of pregnancy, although that was never officially voiced. The restriction was loosened during World War II since most men were at war and continued to be relaxed following the war. William I. Heard, the son of an Iselin coal miner, was a notable exception to the paucity of male elementary school teachers, having taught in elementary schools in Coal Run, McIntyre, and Iselin in the early 1930s before embarking on his career as a chemistry teacher at the high school and collegiate levels. Another exception was Mr Zuchelli, teacher of the 4th grade class of Iselin Elementary School in 1965-66.

When Iselin's grades 7 and 8 were moved to a regional junior high school built in nearby Elders Ridge, a "descendent" of the Elders Ridge Academy, a rec room for civic activities and teen dances was established in one of the three original Iselin Elementary School buildings and a popular ballfield was added. There was a paucity of children's bicycles due to the cost, but "free-range" play abounded among the children. In earlier decades "Splash Day" was celebrated once a year when children would hide in the bushes and throw water on unsuspecting passersby. Charmingly innocent mischief. But mostly days were filled with well-behaved children loving their sleepovers; their raucous games of tag and hide & seek; their "wienie roasts" magically lit by fireflies; their pets; the forts they built in the nearby woods—some of them elaborate structures like the one the boys built in the 1930s using dozens of trees they cut and stripped; their tree-climbing competitions; their swims in the "cricks" (mostly just the boys) and in a swimming hole they dug out in the 1940s; their imaginative burying of "treasure" (pennies in a wooden box in one instance) intended to be found 100 years later; their daredevil sled rides down the steepest hill in town—the infamous Store Hill; their pickup games of football and basketball and, most loved, the pickup games of baseball they played in imitation of Iselin's amazing league players, down to the last detail of posture and attitude and spitting. If it sounds like classic Norman Rockwell America, it was for the children except for the water and air and sanitation hardships they shouldered along with their parents.

"I taught myself to ski, strapping on heavy hand-made wooden skis with a single leather strap, practicing by skiing from the top of Pear Tree Hill down to Red Dog Road in our moderately hilly yard before graduating to Matlack Hill—which was terrifying! I don't remember ever telling my parents I did that. Pear Tree Hill to Matlak Hill was the sum total of my skiing career."

"Skiing became a passion for me. I learned in my yard, then moved to various yards and places like the Store Hill and Matlack Hill. I have skied all over the U.S., Western Canada, and Europe. Those years I moved back to PA after retirement I was a ski instructor for nine years at Blue Knob. I never imagined my childhood dreams would come to fruition. Of course, my dreams were simple, and I feel fortunate to have at least tried to achieve most of them."

"There were lots of kids [living in Iselin] in the 50's and 60's; there were always boys and girls around to play a game of pick-up baseball, basketball, football or my favorite track meet. Everyone knew each other, which was good and bad but it was generally a friendly place to live and lots of activities to keep us all busy."

"When I was just 6 years old and my brother was 3, my mother had to be taken to a nearby sanatorium to be treated when she contracted TB. After a year my father asked some relatives in another state to take care of us since there was no childcare in Iselin and he had to work at his job in the mines. Our mother died after spending two years in the sanatorium. When we returned to live with our father in Iselin in 1941, I didn't get to play much since I had to do all the chores and have dinner on the table when he came home from the mines. I did attend Iselin Elementary School again but dropped out of school in the 9th grade since the bus home from Elders Ridge High School arrived in Iselin too late in the afternoon for me to get my work done. No one thought much about my scrubbing the laundry on a washboard in the tub and cleaning the house and outhouse and buying all the groceries, preparing all the meals, and keeping the kitchen washed up. It was I who took my little brother to the company doctor when he was doing poorly; he was diagnosed with rickets due to his poor nutrition, which fortunately we were able to treat. We all just did what we had to do. But I have been a lifelong learner, taking classes and reading on my own. Some say that I more than caught up with the education I missed to take care of my father and my brother."

"I remember falling asleep in the summertime and along with the breeze coming through the screen in our bedroom window were the heavenly sounds of the Iselin guys—Bob Knopick and Richard Chelednick and their friends-- sitting down on the bridge, a favorite "hangout" near our home, singing in beautiful harmony. *The Yellow Rose of Texas* was one of their favorites."

"In the 1940s and 1950s my father got 98 cents a ton for coal he picked or dug. If the coal was blasted, they got 50 cents a ton. If they got paid in coal company 'script' or currency, that could only be spent in a Company Store that mining companies owned and operated."

In fact, no privately owned retail store was allowed by R&P to be established within the Iselin town limits. But by the 1940s, Iselin residents were blessed by two families establishing "convenience stores." Henry and Alma Gasperini's "mom and pop" store was located just about a half mile out of town at what was called the "Y," so it was walkable. Julia Werner's store was also located at the Y and when it burned down, she was able to build a lovely, bigger store now run by her daughter, Julia on a good lot just a little farther down State Rt 3023 towards Clarksburg. To buy gas or get their car looked at, residents went to see Tony at the Sunoco Station in Clarksburg—all of these stops were within 2 miles of Iselin.

"Also at the Y was the UMWA Union Hall and every Christmas our parents would walk all of us Iselin kids down to get our treats—an orange and a popcorn ball for each of us. Some years if the Union had a little more money to spend, each of us would get a big coloring book and 6 crayons. Mr McCullough dressed up as Santa, but we all knew it was him! This was in the 1950s." She and her siblings were also given one gift from their parents each Christmas; they loved being allowed to choose what it would be.

"I owe my soul to the company store" was not a hyperbolic lyric for the song, *Sixteen Tons*, that Merle Travis wrote and recorded in the 1940s; it was based on actual experiences of coal miners who were members of his Kentucky family. (A second recording by Tennessee Ernie Ford reached #1 in the Billboard charts in 1955.

See https://www.youtube.com/watch?v=2zE1-48AAYc)

Lyrics by Merle Travis

Some people say a man is made outta mud
A poor man's made outta muscle and blood
Muscle and blood and skin and bones
A mind that's a-weak and a back that's strong

You load 16 tons, what do you get?
Another day older and deeper in debt
St. Peter, don't you call me 'cause I can't go
I owe my soul to the company store

I was born one mornin' when the sun didn't shine
I picked up my shovel and I walked to the mine
I loaded 16 tons of number nine coal
And the straw boss said, "Well, a-bless my soul"

You load 16 tons, what do you get?
Another day older and deeper in debt
St. Peter, don't you call me 'cause I can't go
I owe my soul to the company store

I was born one mornin', it was drizzlin' rain
Fightin' and trouble are my middle name
I was raised in the canebrake by an ol' mama lion
Can't no high toned woman make me walk the line

You load 16 tons, what do you get?
Another day older and deeper in debt
St. Peter, don't you call me 'cause I can't go
I owe my soul to the company store

If you see me comin', better step aside
A lotta men didn't, a lotta men died
One fist of iron, the other of steel
If the right one don't get you
Then the left one will

You load 16 tons, what do you get?
Another day older and deeper in debt

St. Peter, don't you call me 'cause I can't go
I owe my soul to the company store

I'm not sure that the coal people of Iselin would agree with being described as having a mind that's a-weak. In fact, I'm sure they would not. And I don't know that many would identify as a fightin' man. And I am certain that many walked the line to earn the love of a high-toned woman. But the central message of the lyrics rings true.

In Iselin, exactly as captured by the song's lyrics, the balance owed at the end of the month tallied in a miner's "book" maintained on a big rack on the wall of the company store was deducted from the individual's paycheck. Some months some miners might receive no cash; some months some might run a deficit and then there was a "discussion" in some homes about who charged what. During one period a token $5 was given to a miner running a deficit on payday. There was evidence of price gouging. And again, the coal company did not allow any privately owned store to open in Iselin, not to sell groceries or hardware or paint or tires or yard goods or seeds or plants or paraffin or pectin or candy or pop or anything. Owning us meant controlling every aspect of the economy of the town.

"The miners all loved John L. Lewis [the President of the United Mine Workers of America from 1920 to 1960]. They hung his photograph in a prominent place on a wall in their homes and hung their hopes for betterment of working and living conditions on him."

The Iselin Navy

The young Angelo Abbati is among the boys gathering materials.

Their Fort. They built things big, just like their dads did for R&P.

Gone Fishin'

Iselin's Little Patriots

Stan Semuskie's 6th birthday party

Pals

Their dads having a good time on the R&P float at the Indiana Sesquicentennial Parade, 1966

Iselin founded in 1903 and we have a Baseball Team in 1906! Unfortunately, the damage to the right side of this vintage photo eliminated two players of this amazing team

Champs. 1940

SOUTHERN SECTION CHAMPIONS

August 17, 1940

Celebrating the Feast of the Assumption, holy day of obligation in all Catholic churches, the Iselin base-
ll team played Coal Run two games as part of the day's festivities Saturday and had reasons to really
lebrate after the afternoon contest, in which Chakan pitched three-hit, shutout ball (7-0), because the ver
ict assured the Ruthowskimen at least a tie for the championship of the Southern Section, Indiana County
eague. The league leaders need only to win one of their remaining four games to "cinch" the pennant.

"The Champions" are (left to right: kneeling—John Molesky, John Petrinig, Geno Beni, Mike Malec,
enry Bosch, Red Ross, Mike Boyda; standing—Frank Cartelli, scorer, Joe Vitkay, Willie Bosch, Joe Bosch,
arry Abbatti, Ben Braeseker, George Chakan, Steve Gordish, Joe Ruthowski, manager, Theodore Gordish,
mpire.

Indiana County Baseball Champions 1941

Indiana County Independent Baseball League Champions for the second consecutive season by virtue of the best-out-of-five series, which
is decided last week-end, are these members of the Iselin Baseball Club; kneeling (left to right)—Batistig, Vitkay, Patrick, Cocovich, H. Bosch,
W. Bosch, Beni; standing—Joe Ruthowski, mgr., Myzwinski, Chakan, Breasecker, Gordish, J. Bosch, Sowinsky, R. Gordish, umpire.

Top: Iselin Baseball Team 1940

Bottom: Iselin Baseball Team 1941

INDIANA EVENING GAZETTE,

THURSDAY, AUGUST 29, 1946.

Iselin Nips Indies Nine By 5-1 Score

The Indiana Indies fell to defeat last evening as the Iselin County League team turned the tables on them by a score of 5 to 1. Semuskie, the Iselinites' hurler, proved to be too much for the locals as he limited them to but four safeties in notching the triumph.

The Iselin aggregation jumped onto starting pitcher Maze of the Indies for four tallys in the third inning for what proved to be the deciding markers of the contest. Andy Stahura scored the Indies only run of the title in the third stanza after he had connected for a two-base clout while Walter Stapleton collected the other three local hits.

The Indies will play host to the Salina nine this evening at the Glassworks Field with the game to start at 6:00.

The box score:

Indiana Ind.	A	R	H
Donnelly, 1	3	0	0
Stapleton, m	3	0	3
Wilden, 1	3	0	0
Hunter, s	3	0	0
Dickie, 2	3	0	0
Maze, p	3	0	0
Stahura, r	3	1	1
Coleman, 3	2	0	0
Zufall, c	2	0	0
Campbell	1	0	0
Totals	25	1	4

Iselin	A	R	H
Bastitic, m	4	1	0
M. Vitkay, s	4	1	0
Maloc, l	3	1	1
J. Vitkay, 2	3	1	1
Patrick, 3	3	0	0
Benl, c	[illegible]	0	0
Gordish, 1	3	0	0
Boyko, r	3	1	1
Semuskie, p	3	0	1
Totals	[illegible]	5	4

Iselin .... 004 000 010—5
Indies .... 001 000 000—1

More than half of the proved oil reserves of the United States are concentrated in Texas.

Top: Iselin Baseball Team
Left: Iselin Baseball Team 1946

Miss Fulton's Class 1914

Alex Semuski's 6th Grade Class 1934

6th Grade Class 1942

2nd Grade Class 1948

Mrs Dezeksky's 3rd Grade Class 1948

Mrs Baker's 1st grade class, 1955

ELDERS RIDGE JOINT SCHOOLS
ISELIN BUILDING

Top: Mrs Baker's 1st Grade Class
Bottom: Mr Zuchelli's 6th Grade Class 1965

Top: Miss Vallosio's 2nd Grade Class 1966
Bottom: Iselin Elementary School's main building, 1984
-abandoned, now torn down

Company Store 1914

Iselin Company Store and attached Post Office

Charlie Pride, Company Store delivery boy 1914

Mine and Doc's Office

Iselin Hotel

Iselin Train Station

WZ3OX Communications

Chapter 12

James P. Lambert (1909-1981)

My father, James P. Lambert was employed by the R&P Coal Company as Town Manager of Iselin in 1941. In the earliest years, the rent for one side of a double unit was $5 to $6 per month. As part of his duties Mr Lambert collected rent from the residents of the miners' housing, which began at $13.25 per month in 1941 and increased gradually to $18.00 per month for a unit in the 1950s and 1960s. Mr Lambert inherited a massive safe from Holy Cross Church when they were upgrading their office; he kept the rent money that he collected and the meticulous records he maintained safely in that safe in advance of his monthly trip to Indiana to turn the money and rent tally over to the owners. The awesome roll top desk came from a barter Mr Lambert made with the exiting occupant, Mr Douglas who said he'd leave the desk if he could take the nice screen door to the front porch. Done! An accomplished carpenter himself, Mr Lambert was in charge of a crew of men employed by R&P to do minimal upkeep and repair to the housing, working out of an R&P-owned Carpenter Shop located on English Street.

“I remember the crew putting up clothes lines for us in our back yards. And once, when I was 6 years old, we had such a big snowstorm that it accumulated to a depth over my head. Six or eight guys from the R&P crew shoveled our [unpaved] roads all over town so we could get out.”

Mr Lambert was able to rent Ms Rosborough's “Big House” from R&P for his young and growing family upon their move from Indiana to Iselin in 1941. During WWII when living space was scarce, the Lamberts welcomed another family to live on the second floor.

It cannot be overstated that the respect Iselin people felt for Mr Lambert was the foundation for his ability to keep a respectable level of law and order in Iselin during his 40 years living there, employed first by R&P and then by Kovalchick as Town Manager. Self-taught in the law, he was a born leader. Elected to serve as Justice of the Peace for Young Township beginning in 1945, he worked at his roll top desk, which was lined with law books, out of his home office in Iselin. His door was always open to air concerns and grievances, and he would take legal action when needed. When a change in the judicial system presented an opportunity to work in a district four times as large as he had been working in, he ran for and won an election to sit as District Magistrate in Indiana County, working out of his office in Blairsville from 1970 until his retirement in 1974, able to serve only 4 of his 6-year term due to poor health.

Another of Mr Lambert’s daughters, my sister Marie writes:

“They called him Mr. Jim, those residents of Iselin and the surrounding area called Young Township. Mr. Jim was one of the few Irish-Americans living in Iselin, the majority of other residents having immigrated from Southern and Eastern Europe. And this was by design. When the Rochester and Pittsburgh Coal Company (R&P) began discovering new veins of coal and building new coal towns, they also needed to recruit a labor force. A letter written in 1902 by Lucius W. Robinson, General Manager of R&P, to a hiring agent in Philadelphia describes the preferred ethnic backgrounds for this work force:

> *We want mainly good Italians, Polanders and Hungarians. We do not want any colored help, or Irish, under any circumstances, nor do we want any hard coal strikers.*
>
> *We do not care for any English-speaking labor being sent here, for it is too apt to be strikers and cast-off labor from other mines.*
>
> *From "McIntyre, Pennsylvania, The Everyday Life of a Coal Mining Company Town: 1910-1947, Copyright Susan Ferrandiz, 2001, www.mcintyrepa.com.*

"This was 1902. The Iselin mine (and many of the other Western Pennsylvania mines owned by the Adrian Iselin family) opened in 1904. The unionization trouble in the late 1800's in the "hard coal" or "anthracite coal" region of Northeastern Pennsylvania was still fresh in the minds of the mine managers. Anyone who spoke or read and wrote English was suspect of becoming a union organizer. And that meant anyone who was Irish, or was in any way related to the Molly Maguires.

> *The Molly Maguires. During the mid-19th century America saw a huge influx of Irish immigrants. Many of these immigrants moved to the anthracite coal regions of eastern Pennsylvania to find work. The Irish*

moved to America hoping they would escape horrible working environments and the brutal tyranny of the English, as well as to find a better life for their families. They soon discovered that the conditions in America were not so different from the conditions in Ireland. They were subject to overwhelming ridicule and discrimination. When searching for work they would see "Help Wanted" signs, but often followed by the words, "No Irish Need Apply." When they were fortunate enough to find jobs, they were working in the most dangerous and horrendous conditions in 19th century America. . . . . Many of the Irish immigrants who relocated to the Anthracite coal region of Pennsylvania originated from oppressed regions of Ireland where the Molly Maguires fought for human rights. It is believed that the Molly Maguires resurfaced in the Pennsylvania coal region in order to fight for the Irish coal miner's rights, but no concrete evidence has ever been obtained to confirm their existence. However, most historians have since accepted their existence as fact.

From "The Legend of the Molly Maguires," by Matt Loy, supplemented by Matthew R. Hengeveld, Copyright 2021, The Pennsylvania State University.

"The culture and nature developed by the Molly Maguires in Ireland was assumed to be the same for whatever name they went by in America. When there were strikes against the coal companies in Northeastern Pennsylvania, both the unions and the coal companies were responsible for numerous violent acts. Eventually 20 men, allegedly Molly Maguires, were hanged in 1877.

"This is the legacy a second-generation Irish-American named James P. Lambert, aged 32, carried with him as he started his employment as Town Manager of Iselin, Pennsylvania. *We do not want any colored help, or Irish, under any circumstances.* Just imagine the courage and determination the job required. But courage and determination were attributes he was never lacking in.

"An examination of just one page of the 1910 United States Census of Young Township, Indiana County, shows the dichotomy of the population at that time. The top half of the page lists the farmers with English or Irish sounding names. Wilkenson, Muckle, Blakeley, Davis and Thomas. They – and their parents - were born in the 1800's in Pennsylvania. They owned their farms. Notice that Lewis Thomas was born in Pennsylvania in 1880 but his parents were born in Wales. Lewis Thomas was listed as an English speaker and his job was Superintendent in the coal mines. He and his wife rented a house.

"The bottom half of the page from the 1910 Census tells a different story. All were born in Italy. Only two heads of households were represented and the rest 'boarders' who worked in the coal mines. All had arrived in America within the last 10 years, so we can hope family members would be sent for, once enough savings could be earned." Marie Lambert McGee, 2022

Oldtimers recall stories of less official law enforcement in Iselin in the 1910s, 1920s, and 1930s than what Mr Lambert was able to establish and maintain as the respected Town Manager and an elected Justice of the Peace and then District Magistrate. One resident remembers being told by her father that a man hired by R&P in those first decades periodically rode a horse through town on a peacekeeping check. "He was authorized by the Coal Company that owned the town during those years [R&P] to enter homes without knocking to make an inspection; he also had the authority to set a curfew for children."

While Iselin coped with its share of rowdy behavior, it was far safer than nearby Whiskey Run. "At the time of its founding, Whiskey Run seemed little different from its parent town of Iselin, five miles away. Whiskey Run came into existence when Iselin mines #1 and #2 expanded due to the great demand for the area's Pittsburgh seam coal, used by railroads for producing steam. Mine #3 was opened, the coal company hurriedly constructed a few 'shanties,' and the town of Whiskey Run was born." Quoting this same article, titled "Whiskey Run: Where Coal Dust Mixed with Murder" and published in *Pennsylvania Heritage* in 1980, "for over 50 years the community of Whiskey Run has been synonymous with violence, secrecy and unsolved murder."

"My grandfather, Thomas Charles Heard, was born in Bristol, England. TC married Lula Florence Henry from Clarion County, PA and his work as a coal miner began in Whiskey Run, PA where his son, my father William Isaac Heard was born in 1909. To escape the notoriously rough and rowdy times in Whiskey Run, TC moved his family when William (Bill) was a boy, re-establishing his work as a coal miner just 5 miles away, in the town of Iselin. When TC was made a Face Boss by the R&P Coal Company, the family moved to a single house on English Street in Iselin."

James P. Lambert (1909-1981)

- ELECT -

JAMES P.

LAMBERT

DIST.
3-3

25
Years
Experience

JUSTICE OF THE PEACE

Left: Mr Jim, Justice of the Peace
Bottom: 1910 U.S. Census for Young Twp, Indiana County

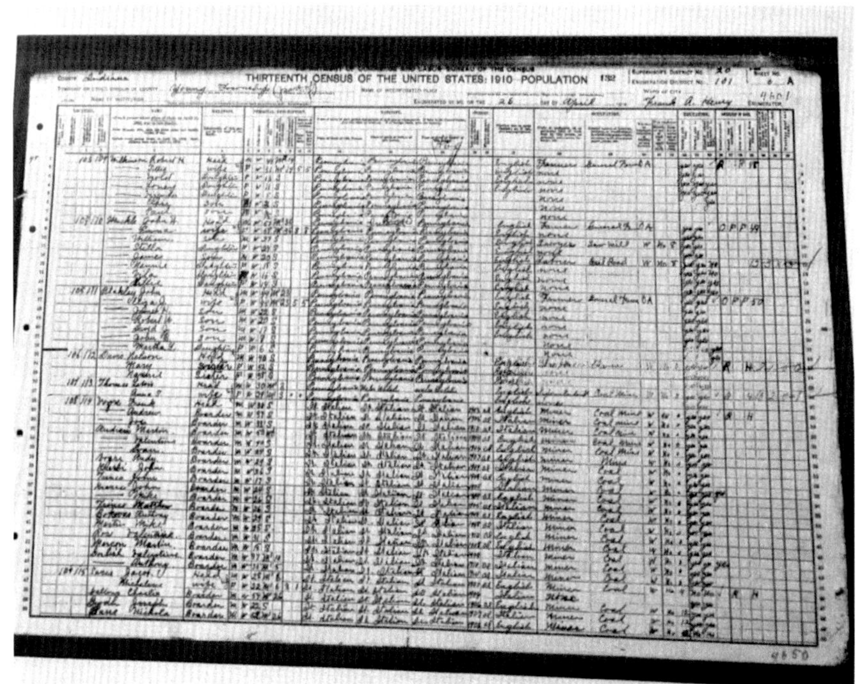

THIRTEENTH CENSUS OF THE UNITED STATES: 1910 POPULATION

Chapter 13

The Kovalchick Era Begins

Nick Kovalchick (1906-1977) made his fortune as the founder in 1928 of the Kovalchick Salvage Company of Indiana, PA, a corporation that he operated throughout the eastern half of the United States. During World War II, President Franklin D. Roosevelt honored the Kovalchick Salvage Company for its major contribution to the war effort. Mr Kovalchick was personally cited for helping to supply and transport scrap and usable steel essential to the Allied effort.

His business is advertised as:

Kovalchick Corporation
Buying and Selling Commercial Scrap Since 1928
"Diversified Business Interests"
Steel*Coal*Railroading*Scrap Yard
Real Estate*Funding

In 1947, Nick Kovalchick formed the Kovalchick Real Estate Division with his purchase of eleven Rochester and Pittsburgh Coal Company mining towns in Indiana, Armstrong, and Jefferson Counties for $890,000, including the purchase of Iselin from R&P. Mr Kovalchick retained Mr Lambert in his capacity of Town Manager of Iselin and allowed him to purchase his home, the "Big House" plus 2 acres of land for $2500 in 1956, paying $31.00 per month "rent to own" option. Mr Lambert must have felt good about that since his parents had never been able to own a home. While the Lambert archives include a statement that as part of Mr Kovalchick's purchase negotiations with R&P Coal Company, he was not allowed to sell Iselin houses for a number of years, no official document was located to verify this statement or reveal the number of years it was in effect and attempts to secure the information from the Kovalchicks went unanswered.

According to Iselin residents, around the mid-1960s Mr Kovalchick did begin allowing Iselin's housing units, which were mostly doubles, to be purchased by individuals, but as originally designed, each had very little land. One oldtimer recalls that the price of one side of a double was $900 and the few single houses that had been built sold for $1000. After receiving title to their home, the new owners made improvements to the extent and on the timetable that their savings allowed. With not enough land to expand, several owners purchased both sides of a double housing unit when that became an option, breaking through walls so that their growing families had more space. Over time they painted or installed aluminum siding on their house and outhouse, painting or wallpapering the inside walls of the outhouse and replacing Sears catalogs and newspaper with commercial toilet tissue, continuing to scrub the inside weekly and to spread lime around the perimeter to lessen the odor. Owners purchased an electric water heater and installed indoor plumbing (tub and/or shower) for bathing when their savings permitted that upgrade. But of course, it was useless to install a toilet for those whose purchase of their home did not include enough land for installing a septic tank and leaching field. The new owners had to continue saving money until they were able to spend more money to purchase a toilet, to pay a plumber for installation and hook up to the sewage system once the piping was installed throughout the town in the mid-1980s, to pay a monthly fee for sewage service, and of course, to undertake the task of safely filling in the hole it left and removing the outhouse from their property or converting it to a toolshed, as some chose to do.

Nick Kovalchick eventually turned over the management of Iselin to his son Joseph, who remains President of the Kovalchick Corporation.

When his job as Iselin's Town Manager was terminated by the Kovalchick Real Estate Division, Mr Lambert was employed as an auxiliary engineer at the Lucerne Power Plant before being elected a District Magistrate in Indiana County in 1970, his last job before retiring from paid employment in 1974.

During this era, the Train Station, Power Plant, and Coal Tipple and the 1903 original housing shacks around the tipple, called Pig's Ear, were torn down. The Iselin Hotel and Rex Theater were torn down leaving an empty lot in the center of town. The Iselin Elementary School was closed and all three of its original buildings plus the nurse's office were torn down. All that remains is just open fields and the ball field. A company doctor was no longer retained to serve the community, that small tile-constructed building with a hipped roof being sold as a private residence as was the adjacent brick Mine Office.

"My grandmother Lambert came from her rented home in Punxsutawney to live with us in the Big House many winters, during the months that it was difficult for her to maintain her coal furnace. Some whole years after R&P no longer employed a company doctor, my father rented the company doctor's house in Iselin for her to live in. We loved that! She taught us how to pick dandelion leaves and fix them in a delicious salad with bacon drippings, and how to play penny ante poker. And laugh til we doubled over! She loved to tell us about earlier days and people she knew and things they did. We'd fold our card hand and get comfortable when she'd stop the card game with 'I mind the time…' I do remember my mother worrying about us little kids walking down to Gramma Lambert's house because it meant our crossing 'Cement Road' with its coal trucks rumbling through town at top speed. Mom would walk out through the alley to the Road with us to monitor our crossing, admonishing us to have Gramma Bess monitor our crossing when coming home. Going to and coming home from Iselin Elementary School required just traversing a safe path over Pear Tree Hill—no monitoring necessary."

The Company Store, located in an imposing brick structure, was eventually closed but the building now houses Iselin's lively volunteer fire department, called the Iselin-West Lebanon Fire Company. According to current residents of Iselin, the excellently trained volunteer firefighters and first responders do a wonderful job responding to structure fires, brush fires, vehicle accidents, and health emergencies. The former Company Store also serves as

Iselin's town hall/polling station as well as a vibrant event center hosting the traditional pizza or wings nights, dances, and holiday parties.

Originally located in this same building and subsequently in a small appendage to the Company Store with its own entrance, Iselin's Post Office had warmly served as a great hub for residents who gathered to pick up their mail and chat with Rachel, the popular Postmistress. When the Company Store was closed, this Post Office was closed, but a Post Office was subsequently opened in a home office on English Street with Steffie, a miner's wife serving as a part-time, also popular Postmistress. There's something about small town post offices being a center for news (with gossip being eschewed by both of these good women), like the hub for news that the old-time phone switchboards became. Eventually this second location was also closed by the USPS. The current residents of Iselin use post office boxes they rent in Clarksburg, 2 miles down Iselin Road, and/or they can receive USPS mail delivery to their home using their Iselin street address and the town of Saltsburg, 15681, which is 7.5 miles from Iselin via PA 286W, as their home address.

R&P sold the town of Iselin and 10 other coal towns to the Kovalchick Real Estate Division in 1947 for $890,000. Thirty years later, R&P donated grants to IUP for three years to support historian and archivist Eileen Mountjoy's research and writing of its history upon its upcoming Centennial in 1981; she also collected many mining artifacts. All of her articles can be found in the IUP archives. With just 6 mines remaining open in Western Pennsylvania, R&P closed its doors after 117 years and sold its entire business to an enterprise headquartered in Pittsburgh, Consolidation Coal Company in 1998, for $150M.

Nick Kovalchick (1907-1977), Indiana, PA

Kovalchick Salvage

More salvage

Endless salvage, adding 11 coal towns in 1947.

Chapter 14

Pursuit of Public Health Improvements for Iselin

Patch town housing was never meant to be permanent housing but just temporary housing for the miners until the vein was tapped out, usually lasting 3-4 decades.

But well into the 1970s, the town of Iselin still had a fair number of residents. However, as noted, the town still had no sewage system and so the houses being rented still had no indoor plumbing, nor did the houses of the new private owners whose purchase did not include enough land to install a septic tank and leaching field. (Modern composting toilets became in common use in the US in the 1970s but were too costly for these residents to purchase.) And the explanation of Iselin's water supply continuing to go dry for weeks and weeks each summer resulting in hazardous health conditions and hardships inflicted on the residents for decades continued to remain a mystery to the residents even as they continued to pay a monthly fee for water. This "drought" happened in all households except for those living on Lower Street; gravity was kind to them, but they say that the taste and smell of sulfur in the trickle of water they did receive during this “dry” period was much worse than usual. For those with no water, it's one thing to haul in drinking/cooking water; it's quite another to have no running water for bathing, washing dishes and cooking utensils, doing laundry and housework, and watering the Victory Gardens. The renters and new owners had to resort to drawing water by hand from the 3 hand pumps (one in the basement of the “Big House,” one near the Doctor's Office, and one centrally located “community” hand pump), area springs, and rainwater collection. Johnson and Johnson was the first company to mass produce disposable diapers in 1948, but that luxury was quite out of reach for most if not all parents of little ones in Iselin. “Taking a bath in a local 'crick' was not uncommon during these dry spells.” “When I was a kid, I wore long sleeve shirts when the water went dry so I wouldn't get dirty, no matter how hot it was!” No containers or hand carts were provided by the owner/landlord to the renters or new owners, whose cartage was often as far as one mile from the water source to their thresholds. Residents of the three “elite” houses (the “Big House,” the Rectory of Holy Cross Church, and the original Mine Foreman's house on English Street) that had a flush toilet but no outhouse had the additional task of hauling buckets of water to those “elite” bathrooms to flush. Judiciously rationing the number of flushes each day to manage the task of hauling buckets of water from the basement to the second-floor bathroom, even when just one toilet accommodated a large family. For weeks and weeks, summer after summer. For decades, lasting until 1981.

Beginning in 1947, the source of water for Iselin's housing units was owned by the Kovalchick Water Company which was formed by Nick Kovalchick concurrent with his forming the Kovalchick Real Estate Division to purchase the housing units in Iselin and in the ten other mining towns in the area from the R&P Coal Company. According to research conducted by Marcia Biederman for her book published in 2021, titled *A Mighty Force*, during the years that Iselin housing stock was owned by R&P followed by the years of ownership by the Kovalchick Real Estate Division and the Kovalchick Water Company, the United Mine Workers of America did not require owners of coal mining towns to supply running water to the homes, but supplying a source of potable water was a requirement of the owners. Providing a hand pump at a well dug at each residence was permissible if the water tested safe to drink by frequent visits from state sanitation inspectors, even if that "safe test" was achieved by the coal company or private owner heavily chlorinating the water in a well that was being polluted by runoff from a privy that was located very close to the well. Similarly, during this period the UMWA did not require owners of coal mining towns to provide indoor toilets with the requisite sewage system but required only that privies be properly maintained, that is, that safe and approved methods of sewage disposal were used, maintaining privies up to the standards set by the PA state sanitation inspectors, verified by frequent testing of the soil surrounding privies.

Residents' ability to live a decent life depended on potable water being dependably supplied to homes in Iselin and depended on soil around the privies being treated if found contaminated in a timely manner so that rains would not disperse the mess the honey dippers invariably left in the alleys into yards where little ones played and into gardens where edibles were grown.

Row of outhouses. When was the soil last tested?
The girl shown reaching down in the photo is Brenda Askins; the two boys are her nephews Shawn and Curtis Askins along with her cousin Kim Wargo.

Chapter 15

Operation Scarlift: The first of three phases of improvements for Iselin achieved by James P. Lambert and colleagues, working as unpaid citizen advocates

Add to this the foul air that hung almost constantly over the town.

Initially administered by the Department of Mines and Mineral Industries and subsequently by the Department Environmental Resources (now Department of Environmental Protection), between 1968 and 1981 the department spent $78M to complete 500 stream pollution abatement projects, and an additional $64M to extinguish 76 underground mine fires, stabilize 156 areas subjected to mine subsidence and prevent air pollution at 28 burning refuse banks.

Mr Lambert was the contact person for Iselin when Operation Scarlift used some of this federal funding to put out the fires in Iselin's boney dumps, thus cleaning up the polluted air in 1974. Still, some old-timers anecdotally report a higher-than-normal incidence of cancer among long-time residents.

To describe that scourge, one man who was born and raised in Iselin, the son of a coal miner, wrote:

"There was another special thing about Iselin, it had a boney pile, which was more of a flat field of black coal that was near the Company Store and close to Lower Street. I guess every mining town had a boney pile but Iselin's was special, it was on fire! Generally, flames were not pushing out of the ground but there was a fire burning underground that constantly spewed out dark gray smoke that filled the air. On clear crisp days one would hardly notice anything about the air, however, on those cold winter mornings when the air was still and didn't move or a warm summer day when the air was thick with fog and moisture, there was a strong smell of burning sulfurous coal.

"I imagine those of us that live there didn't think much about it because along with the burning boney dump as we called it, almost every house had a coal furnace and smoke was thick throughout the town. In winter the two created a very strong acrid smell that permeated the whole town. Many mornings as we walked to school or the bus, we would talk to each other about the smell. Occasionally when I would get on the bus for ERHS [Elders Ridge High School], someone from another town would say, 'Wow, the smell is pretty bad in Iselin today'

"The burning slag coal was often a curiosity and occasionally when we were feeling very brave, we would walk across the burning field of fire and see the cracks in the ground and as we approached and braved to peek down you could see the hot pink glow of a coal fire burning below. I am not sure if anyone ever had an accident, but it could have happened as the ground felt spongy and soft under foot. We would occasionally throw a stick or some paper in to see if we could get a flame to shoot out above ground.

"The burning boney pile was a fact of life in Iselin, from my earliest memories I recall the smell. I left for the Navy in 1967 and much to my surprise 6 years later when I returned to my hometown there was no longer that sulfur smell permeating everything. The terrible scar of the burning boney pile had been extinguished by the US Government, in their attempt to clean up old mining towns. As I recall, all that remained was a field that appeared to have a yellow foam over it. The work that was done was called Operation Scarlift and I can say for sure that all those involved in extinguishing that open sore on Iselin have my thanks. Jim Lambert was a key member of that team of people, coordinating efforts to make Iselin a better place to live... My thanks go out to all who contributed to that effort." Stan Semuskie, 2022

And from another who grew up in Iselin:

"When we left the comfort and familiarity of Iselin Elementary School to attend Junior High and High School in Elders Ridge, which were regional schools, we were very shy, always worrying that the other kids could smell the Iselin boney dump on our clothes and in our hair."

Are Sulphur fumes harmful?

"Inhalation: **VERY TOXIC, can cause death**. Can cause severe irritation of the nose, throat, and eyes. At high concentrations: can cause life-threatening accumulation of fluid in the lungs (pulmonary edema). Symptoms may include coughing, shortness of breath, difficult breathing and tightness in the chest."

"High concentrations of sulfur dioxide can...aggravate existing heart and lung diseases. Exposure to low levels of SO_2 over a long period depletes the respiratory system's ability to defend against bacteria and foreign particles. Particularly sensitive groups include children, the elderly, people with asthma, and those with heart or lung disease."

"Particulate matter (soot), which produces haze can cause chronic bronchitis, aggravated asthma, and premature death (both sulfur dioxide and nitrogen oxides transform into particulates in the atmosphere)." *Union of Concerned Citizens*

"Hard work never hurt nobody" is a phrase I remember hearing as a child, and while it is likely true, in Iselin there were serious hazards that hurt almost everybody, our air quality being one such hazard until the fires below the surface of the boney dump were finally extinguished through Operation Scarlift in 1974.

While this chapter begins to address the negative impact the coal industry had on the health of miners and their families in one small patch town, readers are directed to research the larger issue of the dangerous and even lethal effects that the coal industry has on the nation and the world. In his August 2022 article titled, "Judge revives Obama-era ban on coal sales from federal lands," Associated Press reporter Matthew Brown writes for the *Columbian* in Billings, MT, "Coal combustion for electricity remains one of the top sources of U. S. greenhouse gas emissions, even after many power plants shut down over the past decade because of concerns over pollution and changing economic conditions." And of course, one could and should continue on to read articles such as "Proximity to fracking sites associated with risk of childhood cancer" in *Yale News*, also published in August 2022, and learn that "Pennsylvania children living near unconventional oil and gas (UOG) developments at birth were two to three times more likely to be diagnosed with leukemia between the ages of 1 and 7 than those who did not live near this oil and gas activity, after accounting for other factors that could influence cancer risk, a novel study from the Yale School of Public Health finds." Which points to the urgent need to explore and develop alternatives to burning fossil fuels. Coal miners that I knew and loved would have been happy to learn a new trade skill to work in an industry that provides a source of energy to America with drastically fewer health hazards for all.

Operation Scarlift, 1974

Chapter 16

The Water Renovation Project: The second phase completed by Mr Lambert and his colleagues on the ICMSA, all unpaid citizen advocates

Overlapping Operation Scarlift, in 1973 the Indiana County Commissioners incorporated Indiana County Municipal Services Authority (ICMSA) under the Pennsylvania Municipal Authority's Act. The Water Authority began its work with a budget of $100,000 and now manages maintaining and expanding their work using a current annual budget of $8.5M.

In one of its first actions, in June 1973 a resolution was made to purchase the Kovalchick Water Company, then serving eleven coal mining communities in the central part of the County, including Iselin. Mr Lambert was appointed to serve as Treasurer of the ICMSA. Already in declining health, he nonetheless seized this opportunity to serve the community he had loved and served since 1941. ICMSA, a group of unpaid citizen advocates, succeeded in funding a new system for Iselin, finally bringing a reliable and adequate source of clean running water to Iselin homes in 1981.

Celebrating the victory

Quoting from *Ribbon-Cutting Ceremony For Water Renovation Project* written by Carl Kologie, Assistant Editor of the *Indiana Evening Gazette*, January 12, 1981:

"Ribbon-cutting ceremonies were held on January 12, 1981 at the coalmining towns of Jacksonville, Lucernemines, and Iselin marking the near completion of the final phase of the $3.9M water renovation project in which five water systems were constructed to serve 11 communities in central Indiana County.

"27.7 miles of distribution lines and new water tanks had been installed.

"Ed Sklar, representing Jacksonville Borough [at the dedication of the water treatment plant in Jacksonville] thanked the Authority and pointed out that they received nothing in return for the many hours and work they devoted to the project. Sklar then cut the ribbon and christened the water treatment plant with the traditional smashing of the champagne bottle. A short ceremony was held by Mike Duffalo, the Authority's Executive Director, dedicating the plant to the late William M. Morris who served on the Authority until his untimely death. Robert Kunkle, Chairman of the Indiana County Municipal Services Authority (ICMSA), noted that this was one of the most expensive systems in the water network. It produces over 150 gallons per minute and the water quality is one of the best in the county.

"At the Lucerne site Chairman Kunkle told the gathering that the large tank there holds over 200,000 gallons of water, having a greater growth potential than all the others. Carlos Stabile of

Lucerne, an Authority member, then cut the ribbon and christened the tank."

And last but not least:

"US Congressman John P. Murtha worked with the Authority in obtaining $4M in federal funds and grants for the project. Congressman Murtha was waiting at the Iselin site when the ICTA [Indiana County Transit Authority] bus carrying 25 persons arrived at 2:15 p.m. on January 12, 1981. Freezing temperatures kept the crowds sparse and the remarks brief. Rev John Healy [sic Hili] of Holy Cross Church, Iselin, offered the invocation at the Iselin site. Jim Lambert, a resident of Iselin and member of the Authority, proposed a toast to all who assisted in making the new water system a reality in Iselin. He then christened the new tank in Iselin with a bottle of champagne. Young Township Supervisors Stanley Bendis, Ben Morgan, and John Steffenino were also in attendance at the Young Township site.

"Indiana County Commissioner William McMillen said this was only the beginning. He noted that the County had assisted in the funding and granted approx. $127,000 to ICMSA. McMillen noted that when this money was returned by the Authority it will be "rolled over" for the same type of projects [water and sewage] in the County.

"Following the three christening ceremonies, a dinner meeting was held at the Holiday Inn in Indiana on Sunday evening with upwards of 100 persons attending. Robert Kunkle was presented a plaque by members of the Authority and was re-elected to his ninth term as Chairman of the Authority. Other officers re-elected on the

Authority included Robert Olson, Vice chairman, Wilbur Stairs, secretary, James Lambert, treasurer, and solicitor Robert Douglass.

"Letters from State Senator Pat Stapleton and State Representative Paul Wass were read, expressing their regrets that they were unable to attend the event and sending their congratulations and appreciation for a complex but important job well done."

Five New Systems Completed

Ribbon-Cutting Ceremony Held For Water Renovation Project

By CARL KOLOGIE
Gazette Assistant Editor

Ribbon-cutting ceremonies were held Sunday afternoon at Iselin, Jacksonville and Lucernemines marking the near completion of the final phase of the $8.9 million water renovation project in which five water systems were constructed to serve 11 communities in central Indiana County.

Final inspections on all five new water systems had been made by representatives of Farmers Home Administration on Dec. 11, 1980, when all the systems were substantially complete and operative.

Bob Kunkle, chairman of the Indiana County Municipal Services Authority (ICMSA), the agency responsible for the project, stated that it was fitting that the ribbon-cutting ceremonies be held on the same day that ICMSA would adopt a resolution authorizing issuance of a bond of $1.25 million for financing of the project.

Following the ceremonies at the three sites a dinner was held at the Holiday Inn where the annual reorganization meeting was held and Kunkle was re-elected to serve his ninth consecutive term as board chairman.

U.S. Congressman John P. Murtha was waiting at the Iselin site when the ICTA bus carrying 25 persons arrived at 2:15 p.m. yesterday afternoon.

Freezing temperatures kept the crowds sparse and the remarks brief.

Murtha complimented Kunkle, the authority and local officials for the work that had been done.

"I worked with the authority in obtaining $4 million in federal funds and grants for the project and this is a prime example of how federal money should be used."

Murtha recalled that the late Bruno Telk of Ernest had approached him with a bottle of dirty water and asked what could be done about the water problem in that area.

"I'm proud to have helped and have been a part of this project," said the congressman.

Indiana County Commissioner William McMillen said this was only the beginning. He noted that the county had assisted in the funding and had granted money to the authority (approximately $127,000).

McMillen noted that when this money was returned by the authority it will be "rolled over" for the same type of projects in the county.

The money has not been incorporated into the county budgetso it will be used by the authority for their work with water and sewage in the county.

Jim Lambert, a resident of Iselin and member of the authority, proposed a toast to all who assisted in making the new water system a reality in Iselin. He then christened the new tank in Iselin with a bottle of champagne.

Young Township Supervisors Stanley Bendis, Ben Morgan and John Steffenino were also in attendance at the Young Township site.

At Jacksonville the ribbon-cutting was held inside the water treatment plant located south of the borough.

Kunkle noted this was one of the most expensive systems in the water network. It produces over 150 gallons per minute and the water quality is one of the best in the county.

Mike Duffalo, ICMSA director, then called Mrs. William M. Morris and her three sons, Jeff, Larry and Denny, as a short ceremony was held to dedicate the plant to the late William M. Morris who served on the authority until his untimely death.

Mrs. Morris and her sons were presented a plaque from the authority and then placed a sign on a tank naming the plant the William M. Morris Plant.

Indiana County Commissioner Jay Dilts thanked the authority for their efforts in seeing the project through to its completion and noted that water is only the beginning and will lead to further development in this area.

Ed Sklar, representing Jacksonville Borough, also thanked the authority and pointed out that they received nothing in return for the many hour and work they devoted to the project.

Sklar then cut the ribbon and christened the building with the traditional smashing of the champagne bottle.

At the Lucerne site Kunkle told the gathering that the large tank there holds over 200,000 gallons of water and this site had a greater growth potential than all the others as it covered an area from just south of Indiana Borough to Coral.

Kunkle said that 27.7 miles of distribution lines had been installed in the new payments of $80,000 per year until the year 2021.

Duffalo then expressed the gratitude of the authority to Kimbell Engineering who designed the project and was on hand to oversee the work until its completion.

He then called upon Mrs. Bruno Telk, her son Bob and her late late husband's sister, Helen Laskey as the site of dedicated to Telk, an authority member from Ernest until he passed away last year.

Indiana County Commissioner Day Nichol then expressed his thanks to all who worked on the project.

Carlos Stabile of Lucerne, an authority member, then cut the ribbon and christened the tank.

Sunday evening a dinner meeting was held at the Holiday Inn with upwards of 100 persons attending.

Kunkle read letters from state Senator Pat Stapleton and state Representative Paul Wass who expressed their regrets they were unable to attend the event.

One of the highlights of the dinner was the presentation of a plaque to Kunkle from ICMSA vice chairman Robert Olson. The plaque was from the members of the authority who paid tribute to Kunkle for this eight years of leadership as chairman.

Duffalo then praised the borough of Ernest.

"I give them credit for taking over operation of their own water system. More power to them if they can operate the system better than the authority. We encourage them to do it."

Ernest had originally been one of the communities involved in the county-wide water system under ICMSA.

The resolution on the $1.25 million indebtedness to the authority was then approved unanimously.

Roland Kolbeck, an executive with Kimball Engineering, reported on the progress of the project and said with the exception of final testing, the operation was nearly completed.

Rev. John Healy of Holy Cross Church, Iselin, offered the invocation at the Iselin site while Rev. Stan Jasonek of St. Gertrude's in McIntyre offered the invocation at the Jacksonville and Lucernemines sites.

Besides Kunkle, other officers re-elected on the authority included Olson, vice chairman; Wilbur Stairs, secretary; Lambert, treasurer; and solicitor Robert Douglass.

Ribbon Cutting Ceremony, *Indiana Gazette* article describing the citation by the ICMSA honoring James P. Lambert for his advocacy and his christening of the Water Tank in Iselin on January 12, 1981.

Gazetteland

TODAY TODAY TODAY TODAY TODAY TODAY TODAY

Indiana Evening Gazette

Monday, January 12, 1981

At Lucernemines Sunday afternoon a ribbon-cutting ceremony was held marking the completion of the water renovation project. In the above photo the old tanks, left, are in contrast to the new 200,000 gallon tank on the right. Officials huddle in the freezing temperatures during the brief ceremony.

Left: Lucernemines Ceremony-*Gazette*
Bottom: ICMSA members, 1981, *Gazette*.
Front Row l to r: James Lambert, Wilbur Stairs, Jack Steffenino (sic), Robert Olson, Tom Spring, and Harry Almes.
Back Row: Carlo Stabile, Mike Duffalo (ED), Robert Kunkle, Art Miller, and Mary Galinac.

Members of the Indiana County Municipal Authority held their annual reorganization meeting Sunday evening. Standing, in the front row from left to right: James Lambert, Wilbur Stairs, Jack Steffinino, Robert Olson, Tom Spring and Harry Almes. Back row: Carlo Stabile, Mike Duffalo, Robert Kunkle, Art Miller and Mary Galinac. All are authority members with the exception of Duffalo, the executive director.

Chapter 17

A Sewage System for Iselin: Phase three realized a few short years after Mr Lambert's passing

A sewage system was brought to Iselin in the mid-1980s that supported the installation of indoor toilets in each unit of a double house and in single houses; this system also serviced Iselin's two Churches and the former Company Store. Although the actual cost of the fixtures and installation fell to the owner of the unit, now at least when they could afford the costs, the owner could hook into a sewage system for which they paid a monthly fee, in addition to paying a monthly fee for water. Renters (not likely to make the investment) continued to use their outhouses, waiting for better conditions to be provided by their owner/landlord.

First, Some Thoughts About Outhouses

It's an interesting word, "outhouse," isn't it? Typically farms and rural homes have one or more "outbuildings" that house tools, equipment, fuel, animal feed, chicken coops and rabbit hutches, washhouses, and even kitchens. But the term "outhouse" seems always to have been designated as the name of the shelter built to protect a pit latrine or privy. Iselin's outhouses were constructed using a centuries-old basic design, one that was/is used around the globe, intended to improve sanitation by separating the handling of human waste from the household. But the "house" in "outhouse" grabs my attention, knowing that in Iselin when residents were able to purchase their duplex or single house from the Kovalchick Real Estate division, many immediately set about painting or installing aluminum siding on their outhouse, painting or wallpapering the interior while keeping up their routine weekly scrubbing and liming. They truly treated their outhouse as an extension of their house, but located at a safe distance from the main living space as kitchens were located in an outbuilding in the earlier centuries as a measure of fire prevention to the main house. Outhouses continue to serve a good purpose in remote areas, including in some of our National Parks, continue serving folks wanting to live off the grid, and continue being used in underdeveloped areas of our global communities. And no, a half moon on the door was not a part of Iselin outhouse design.

Thomas Jefferson had enjoyed the luxury of flush toilets in the Paris townhouse he rented in the late 1700s, but this luxury took decades to reach his home in Virginia, and almost two centuries to reach homes in Iselin.

"And with regard to English conveniences, they are also an unknown luxury in the United States, where there are only "little houses" five hundred paces from the house whenever possible. That is very disagreeable in winter with the snow, and in summer when summer complaint, diarrhea, is quite a common ailment. Irénée has done an extraordinary thing for me with a 'little house' twenty-five paces away in a little thicket; and when it rains I should like it better even closer. In Washington, Madam Barlow placed hers at the end of the piazza; that is a great improvement. But that lady has French manners. At Monticello, Mr. Jefferson's home, one has the choice of three hundred paces in the garden and on the terraces or through an underground tunnel, level with the cellars and built for that purpose."

– Pierre S. du Pont de Nemours to his wife, September 28, 1816

The search for a safe way of handling human waste is as old as civilization itself.

"As early as 15 centuries before Christ, the Old Testament (Deuteronomy 23:12-13) offered this practical advice: 'Designate a place outside the camp where you can go to relieve yourself. As part of your encampment, have something to dig with, and when you relieve yourself, dig a hole and cover your excrement.'

"Eventually, mankind's formation into communities brought about the need for greater privacy. In the Neolithic Scottish settlement of Skara Brae, some Stone Age huts had stone seats with a hole in them and drainage to the outside. Ancient Egypt had similar 'furnishings,' though the seats were limestone for the well-to-do and wooden for the less fortunate. Ancient China probably deserves credit for providing the first outhouses, private enclosures removed from homes or businesses to provide privacy, keep unpleasant odors away from living areas and improve sanitation. In later times, the outhouse was sometimes called a 'privy,' an abbreviated form of the word 'privacy.'

“Around 4500 B.C., the first collection system for human excrement was constructed by the Romans, who were among the first to build sewers underneath street level to collect both rain water and sewage. Nevertheless, conditions remained quite primitive overall, with a communal sponge on a stick being used in lieu of toilet paper.”

“Many centuries passed without significant improvements in methods for dealing with human excrement. In Medieval times, “garderobes” were often incorporated into castle walls; these were toilet rooms which discharged directly into the moat below, creating a cesspool. Warning cries of “gardez l’eau” (“Watch out for the water!”) would be shouted by those using these facilities. “L’eau” eventually became the source of today’s reference to a toilet as “the loo.” Ironically, garderobe is the French word for “wardrobe,” since clothing was sometimes stored in the garderobe because the stench kept moths away, according to Linda Manwiller [a researcher who is a resident of Stouchsburg, Berks County, Pa]. --Sue Bowman, *Pondering the Privy—A History of Outhouses*, writing for *Lancaster Farming.*

Unpleasant odor and privacy seem to be issues of higher concern in periods before medical science began to teach us the danger of typhoid and a host of intestinal infectious diseases such as schistosomiasis “and other diseases associated with poverty,” specifically through the seepage of waste into the soil from outhouse foundations.

In olden times, a latrine pit was simply abandoned when it filled up, moving the “outhouse” over a newly dug pit and covering the old pit with dirt, just as advised in Deuteronomy 23:12-13 seventeen centuries ago.

The housing stock built in Iselin in 1903 was never meant to be permanent housing but rather, was expected to be abandoned when the mine for that vein of coal was closed. Similarly, Iselin's outhouses were never expected to be in use for more than 3 or 4 decades, that is, just into the 1930s or 1940s.

Where the intended "improvement of sanitation by separating human waste from the household" breaks down in the coal town of Iselin is in the condition of the foundations due to their age being past their "expiration date" and in the concentration of so many outhouses in such a small amount of space. What action, then, is called for in the 1980s, a whole generation later?

It is annoying when people chime in on this topic with nostalgic memories of using their grandparents' outhouse or perhaps even memories of having grown up on a farm with no indoor plumbing.

I, too, have fond memories of the outhouse my father built for our fishing camp, our beloved Camp Shamrock. He never warned us of dangerous health hazards when using our single outhouse that had been carefully built and well-maintained in the wilderness. Mostly we children were cautioned to be on the lookout for rattlesnakes and an occasional bear.

"Put on your thinking caps," as our Iselin Elementary School teachers used to preface a "think it through" session with us. There is a huge difference between the obvious inconvenience of having to use an outhouse that had been "carefully built and well-maintained" in the wilderness or on a farm or an estate such as Monticello, a huge difference between that inconvenience and the deadly health hazard created when an alley separated four duplex houses on the right from four duplexes on the left side of the alley. That created sixteen outhouses lining the alley, all in very close proximity ("very" and "close" being modifiers used, although they are redundant to "proximity," to emphasize just how close the outhouses were to each other). This describes the patchwork of alleyways all over the town of Iselin.

Unrelenting

James P. Lambert was already enjoying the victories earned when he and his fellow unpaid citizen advocates used Operation Scarlift funding in the 1970s to put out the fires in the boney dumps, eliminating those dangerous noxious fumes from Iselin's air. And then he felt great joy as he celebrated with the other unpaid members of the Indiana County Municipal Services Authority when, using county, state, and federal grants, they were able to purchase Iselin's water supply from the Kovalchick Water Company and bring in a reliable and adequate source of potable running water to the entire town, dedicating the new water tower in January 1981.

But what would Mr Lambert do about the deadly health hazard that the concentration of outhouses with their outdated and unsafe foundations presented to his neighbors? His health was failing and his own family was safe, having clean air and plenty of potable running water and an indoor toilet serviced by a new septic tank and leaching field they were able to install for their home in the 1950s since along with their purchase of the "Big House" came two acres of land.

His acceptance of his reappointment as a member and Treasurer of the Indiana County Municipal Services Authority in January 1981, however, signaled that Mr Lambert was not about to walk away from the issue, a social justice issue that was, in his mind, of great importance to the wellbeing of the people of Iselin, an issue that stubbornly remained on his personal list as unacceptable. He was simply not able to stop at having contributed substantially to establishing and maintaining law and order, good education, safe air to breathe, and universal access to potable water for the coal people and their families who were his lifelong friends and neighbors.

Would he advocate for funds to rebuild the foundations under the outhouses that were crumbling and leaking, having been built in 1904 and never updated? Surely he was aware of what Sue Bowman went on to describe in her 2022 article *Pondering the Privy*: "First Lady Eleanor Roosevelt played an important role in improving sanitation in the countryside. Under the Work Projects Administration, during Franklin D. Roosevelt's presidency, three-man WPA work teams replaced old outhouses in rural areas. They could build one in 20 hours at a cost of $5 that included concrete floors and screened ventilation. Over 2 million such outhouses were built by the WPA. Eleanor Roosevelt's championing of the WPA outhouse reconstruction program coined two more nicknames for outhouses, the 'Eleanor' and the 'White House.'"

Would he advocate the town's owner to provide more frequent trips from the "honey dippers" and less slop left in the alleys after they did their servicing of the outhouses, which invariably was washed by rain into the yards where children played and into the gardens where edibles were grown by the residents?

Would he advocate for regular visits from state inspectors to test the soil around the outhouses?

Would he advocate for enforcing fines on owners who did not comply with state safety standards?

Would he advocate for setting higher state safety standards?

Oh no. James Lambert was done with all of this. Done with seeing the hardships and deadly health hazards created by such a concentration of outhouses jammed into his neighbors' living spaces. They knew him well and admired his ability to envision a solution and work through complexities, never settling for a Band-Aid fix, never losing patience to get it right. He would quietly advocate for a sewage system for Iselin, knowing (but never acknowledging) that he would probably not live to see it completed.

Sewage Demonstration Project: The First Step

It would take several stages to get a sewage system in place to make it possible for all the residents of Iselin finally to have indoor flushing toilets. The system that was proposed for Iselin was designed and constructed by the Pennsylvania Department of Environmental Resources and the first milestone was marked by the Dedication of the Sewage Demonstration Project in the Summer of 1982, a little over a year after the passing of James Lambert.

Photos from the Lambert family photo album show the joyful groundbreaking ceremony conducted by Mike Duffalo, the ED of the Indiana County Municipal Services Authority and members of the ICMSA in the Summer of 1982. Mr Lambert's widow, Sara was presented a plaque by Mr Duffalo in appreciation of her late husband's advocacy.

Many Iselin residents attended the ceremony, held on Lower Street near the old Company Store at the point of "influent" of waste to the proposed sewage treatment plant in Iselin's marsh/pond/meadow. It is interesting to note that the land that was used was the very land that Operation Scarlift turned from a smouldering boney dump into fertile soil a decade earlier.

Not all of the Lamberts' five adult children could attend the groundbreaking ceremony, but their son, the late James M., was there with his wife and four children. And their eldest daughter, the late Jane Lambert Abe, and her late husband and two children flew in from Salt Lake City to celebrate her father's final achievement in his quest for social justice for the beloved residents of his beloved town.

And typical of the Lambert spirit, after the ceremony an Open House was held at the Big House, attended by many Iselin residents as well as Lambert friends and relatives who came together from all over Indiana County. Shooting hoops was a typical intergenerational activity at their gatherings.

His unrelenting (and unpaid) citizen advocacy for social justice was a source of great pride for the family of James P. Lambert as well as for the residents of Iselin and for his colleagues in Indiana County.

Knowing that reading in this book about his fine attributes and bold actions inspires a new generation of citizen advocates would be the legacy most cherished by James P. Lambert—a legacy of inspiration.

SUCCESS

After the construction of the Iselin Artificial Treatment Scheme in the Summer of 1982, a little over a year after Mr Lambert's passing, as illustrated in Figure 1, trenches had to be dug and pipes had to be laid throughout the town. Unfortunately, no photographs of this phase have been located to date but there is mention of the digging of trenches for Holy Cross Church to connect to Iselin's Rural Waste Water Plant in their *Diamond Jubilee (1908-1983)* booklet.

The success of the proposal was documented just a couple of years later when it was picked up by the Tennessee Valley Authority as a model of the use of a marsh/pond/meadow system or treatment of municipal wastewater as a low-cost system for meeting stringent National Pollutant Discharge Elimination System discharge limitations. In 1986 the TVA's Office of Natural Resources and Economic Development presented a paper titled "Design and Performance of the Artificial Wetlands Wastewater Treatment Plant at Iselin, Pennsylvania" to the Conference on Research and Applications of Aquatic Plants for Water Treatment and Resource Recover held in Orlando, FL in July 1986 and again in Chattanooga, TN that same month. Quoting their Introduction: "Small communities nationwide are having extreme difficulties in providing affordable wastewater disposal that will meet state and federal water quality regulations. Conventional and 'high-tech' methods are generally too expensive to construct and operate." The report continues, "The treatment facility serves 158 of the 300 residents of Iselin. It consists of six components in series: pretreatment, an aeration cell, a cattail marsh, a stabilization pond, a reed canary grass meadow, and a chlorination unit," which is sketched in Figure 1 Iselin Artificial Wetland Treatment Scheme.

All of this research and work for only 158 residents, you may ask. For Mr Lambert that was the end of a lifetime of hardship and dangerous health hazards endured by 158 friends and neighbors, with the possibility of the remaining 142, probably all renters, having a chance to be brought online by their landlord. Cause for real celebration.

In 1994 the Indiana County Municipal Services Administration continued its work, winning a grant from the Pennsylvania Department of Community and Economic Development to bring the Pond Marsh Pond Replacement Project to Iselin.

Iselin townspeople attending the Dedication

Groundbreaking for the Sewage Demonstration Project

Michael Duffalo, ED of the ICMSA speaking to the gathering

Presentation of a plaque to Sara, the widow of James P. Lambert, surrounded by 2 of their 5 children and 6 of their 15 grandchildren

Mrs Lambert and her daughter Jane, son-in-law Clifford, and their children Susan and Bruce Abe, in front of the Big House

Open House at the Big House following the Dedication

The requisite game of hoops was always intergenerational.

One of Jefferson's outhouses at Monticello

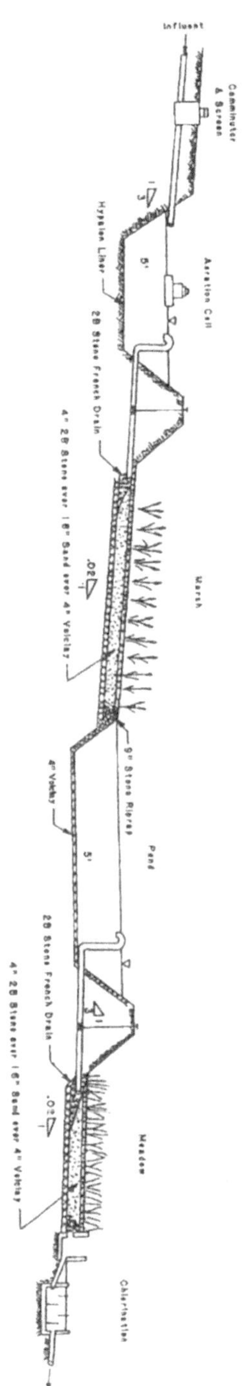

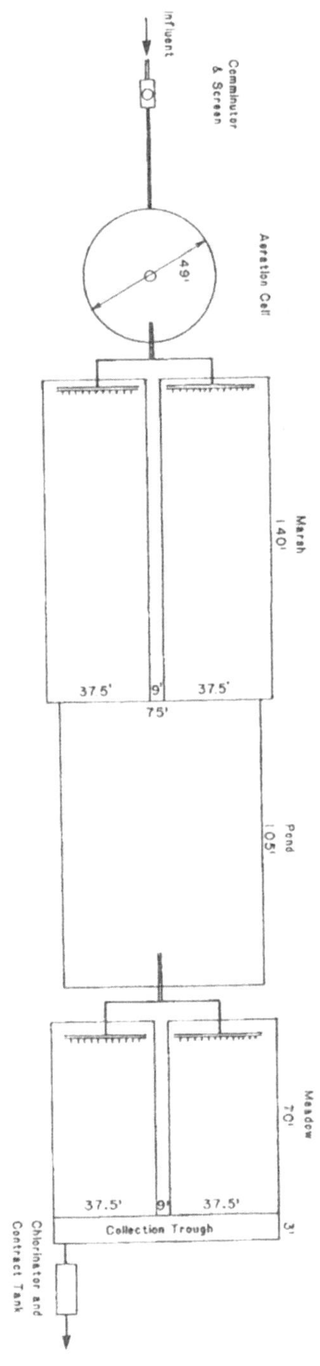

Figure 1. Iselin Artificial Wetlands Treatment Scheme

Left: Figure 1. Iselin Artificial Wetlands Treatment Scheme
Top: Iselin Marsh Pond Replacement Project, 1994

Chapter 18

The Iselin Lamberts

My parents, James P. Lambert and Sara L. Lambert lived in Iselin where they raised us five children beginning in 1941, my father from 1941 until his passing in 1981—almost exactly the middle third of the 120-year history of Iselin that this book narrates—and my mother from 1941 until her move to live with one of her daughters, my sister Marie in Vermont in 2015.

At her husband's passing, Mrs Lambert was able to receive a widow's pension from the miners' union (UMWA) as well as a supplemental pension through an Act signed into law by President Reagan, H.R. 5159, which contains the Black Lung Benefits Revenue Act of 1981, while she shared the worry and pain with many if not all of the Iselin miners and their families and their Town Manager, her husband, who was never required to go down into the pits but who nonetheless did not evade the suffering and the heartache of this terrible Black Lung disease as a surface worker. Bituminous coal underground mining employs slightly more than half of all coal mining industry workers, but experiences a higher share of occupational injuries, illnesses, and fatalities. In a study completed by the US Bureau of Labor Statistics, the average life expectancy in the coal mines for those starting work at 15 years of age was found to be 49.23 years underground workers and 58.91 years for surface workers. The hazards in the pits include being directly exposed to toxic fumes, coal dust and toxic metals, acid mine drainage, lack of sunlight, hearing loss, plus the threat of being crushed, drowned, or injured from fires or being trapped for indefinite periods of time by a structural collapse. To give a sample statistic, during the 6-year period from 1915 to 1921, 222 miners died in Indiana County coal mines, almost one per week county-wide deaths. An explosion in the Iselin mines in 1940, the year before the Lamberts arrived in Iselin, took the lives of several beloved Iselin coal miners. It is remembered that the fiancée of one of those killed suffered what was called a nervous breakdown. Even non-lethal issues took a toll on the miners' bodies.

“I've mined coal in places two feet tall. I could barely take a drink of water; you'd have to pour it in sideways. When you were in places four feet high, why you thought you was in heaven.”

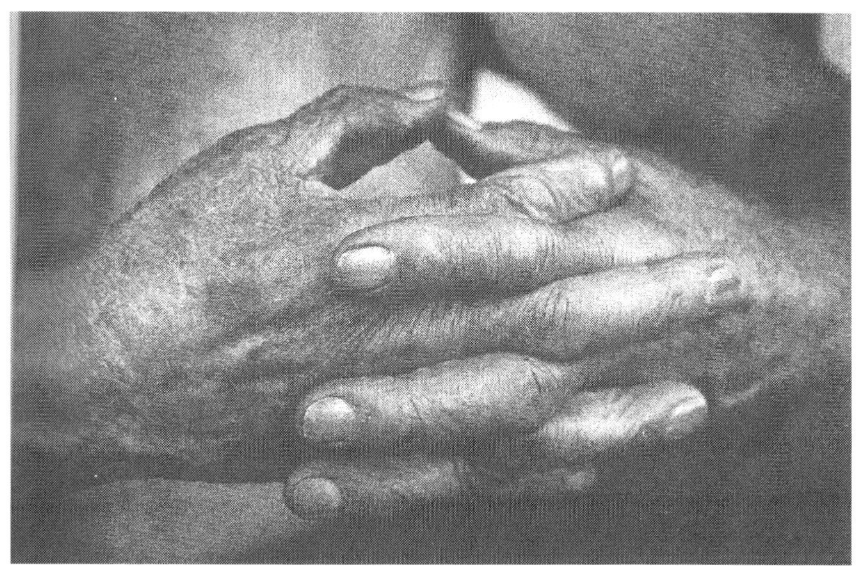

The hands of Rudolph Gordish, Iselin coal miner who said in an interview for Coal People, "I went to PIT--not Pittsburgh University --but down under, you know what I mean. I lost a hell of a lot of sunlight down there."

Mrs Lambert was a 1927 graduate of Sandy Township High School in DuBois PA following an academic track curriculum, and a 1929 graduate of Indiana Normal School which was subsequently expanded to become Indiana University of Pennsylvania, located in Indiana PA just 17 miles northeast of Iselin. Named a member of IUP's Pioneer Society in 2014, she lived on in the "Big House" in Iselin to the age of 105, after which she spent one year living with one of her daughters in Vermont until her passing in 2016. Mrs Lambert was active as a teacher in the Iselin Elementary School, a member of Holy Cross Church, a volunteer for the March of Dimes, and a volunteer to distribute cheese, dried beans, peanut butter, and other federal surplus items to those in need in Iselin. She fed her family with vegetables and strawberries and delicious rhubarb from her well-tended Victory Garden, fruit from her pear, cherry, apple and plum trees and her grape vines and berry bushes, all managed by her harvesting/canning skills. In addition to food from her robust chicken coop, she supplemented these resources with wild game that her husband brought home from his hunting trips with his brothers and later with his sons and trout that she and her husband and children brought home, thanks to their active love of these outdoor sports. Neighboring farmers delivered milk and delicious sausage at reasonable prices. Some of the Iselin families also kept rabbits and a few kept a cow to supplement their diets.

"I can state unequivocally that no Iselin resident suffered from chronic hunger."

While her flower gardens were not opulent, oldtimers still fondly remember Mrs Lambert nurturing her small bed of tulips and delicate lilies of the valley under a hundred-year-old lilac tree, her sentimental dogwood tree that she planted on Pear Tree Hill, her treasured heritage shamrock plants, climbing roses, and glorious Resurrection lilies, and her rhododendron bushes that dramatically grew to roof-line height. Inside, her stunning array of African violets flourished on a windowsill that was extraordinarily deep due to the construction of the "Big House" as described in Chapter 22 of this book; she had chosen the one sill that was not only deep but had the proper exposure to the sun for these plants. Mrs Lambert had a deep appreciation for classical music. Having taken piano lessons beginning in her childhood, she performed such classics as Beethoven and Schubert Sonatas as well as accompaniments for her brother Lee, who played the classical violin repertoire with her in recitals held in DuBois, PA throughout their youth. She loved the violin music of Fritz Kreisler. She also loved old favorites which she played for songfests with her family gathered around the piano in Iselin. She played for friends during the month of her 100th birthday—and later! For almost 50 years Mrs Lambert belonged to a bridge club with seven ladies who lived in Indiana. They met monthly, sharing stories of their children and their lives, her friends making the trip "out to Iselin" when it was her turn to host, a cause for bringing out the good glassware and dishes on which to serve delicious desserts. What her children remember most was being relegated to other parts of the house to remain quiet, but each was allowed one small bottle of the Coca Cola that was purchased for the occasion, a rare treat. They giggled as they sipped, playing "fancy."

Together Sara and James Lambert served the community during the air raids of WWII by devising a warning-all clear system during mandatory blackouts, and offered neighbors use of their telephone for decades until more were able to install a telephone in their home. Their home was filled with love and laughter and music…and neighbors and relatives who came to them for help or just to visit!

"My mother loved the big house in Iselin. She thought it was the most peaceful place and she thought the people of Iselin were the best people in the world. And they loved her too."

James P. and Sara (Hayes) Lambert's formal wedding photograph, 1936

Sara L. Lambert (1909-2016)

Chapter 19

A Family's Devotion to Public Health

Grants or Courts? Sara L. Lambert's great uncle, Dr Leo Z. Hayes, was a beloved and devoted company doctor, employed by the Shawmut Mining Company in Force, PA, a coal town 80 miles northeast of Iselin but familiar to Sara since it is located just 18 miles north of DuBois, PA where both she and her husband had grown up. Even as Dr Leo lay dying in December 1942, he worried about his patients. Wartime had created a severe shortage of civilian physicians, particularly in rural areas. Caring for miners and their families, Leo was the only physician within a twenty-five-mile radius with four thousand inhabitants. In a scene later memorialized by Woody Guthrie in his song, *The Dying Doctor,* Dr Leo asked his eight children, five of whom had earned a medical degree, to assure him that one of them would continue to take care of the miners. The job fell to Elizabeth, his youngest, who was Sara's first cousin once removed.

Woody wrote down the compelling lyrics but unfortunately never wrote down or recorded the song, if he indeed wrote one, which remains unknown:

https://www.woodyguthrie.org/Lyrics/Dying_Doctor.htm

The Dying Doctor
Words by Woody Guthrie

Doctor Leo Hayes was our company doctor
From the big coal companies he got his pay
For thirty-nine years he tried to cure us
And now today on his deathbed lay.
He called his five boys and his three daughters
And at his bed we stood around
We heard him tell the history of the coal miners
And he said, "Don't let these people down."

You are all connected with the practice of medicine
You promise you'll keep true I know
You will do your best to help these people
I close my eyes for I must go.
His youngest girl was Doctor Betty
With her face so pretty and her smile so sweet
She walked the coal towns of Force and Byrndale
She saw the sewage waters flowing down the street.

She saw the children drink the cankered water
She saw the chickens fly up on the roof
She saw the waters overflow the sewers
And flood their gardens of victory.
She went to the big shots of the Shawmut Company
She did not beg and she did not plead
She stood flatfooted and pounded the table
Sewer pipes and bathrooms are what we need.

My dady (sic) told me to fight to cure sickness

But I can't cure sickness with sewage all around
These germs kill people quicker than I can cure them
We need a foundation under every house.
We need a bathroom for every family
Yes, you can set there and blink your eyes
Three hundred miners are out behind me
We will clean this town or know the reason why.

I quit my job as the family doctor
I nailed up my shingle and went on my own
I carried my pillbag and waded those waters
I set by a deathbed in many a home.
I saw you catch rainwater in rusty washtubs
I saw you come home dirty up out of your pits
Watched you ride with your coffin up to your graveyard
With not a nickel to pay your burying debt.

On July the fifteenth from the hills around
Three hundred miners walked down through town
The state inspector was testing the water
While he was working you stood around.
One miner asked him to have a drink free
The inspector looked out toward our pits
He set his hat back on his head and says,
"I wouldn't drink a drop of that on a bet."

I think of my daddy and brothers and sisters
When we stood around his dying bed
When I walk the streets of the company towns
I can hear every word my daddy said.
The Shawmut Company is caught in its own paws
The people not worth the money they cost
A hundred have died, three hundred not working
Thirty thousand tons of coal is lost

After succeeding her father as company doctor (overcoming opposition from the Shawmut Coal Company that did not want another uncontrollable, integrity-driven Hayes and certainly did not want a woman), Elizabeth Hayes (1912-1984), who earned her MD degree with honors at Temple University School of Medicine in 1936, drew widespread attention in 1945 for protesting the unsanitary conditions in Force.

"A suspected case of typhoid leads Hayes to pay for private testing of the wells. As she suspects, the water is contaminated. And it is no wonder, since Shawmut neglected to maintain the outhouses.

"As a result, rainstorms caused feces to flow down streets and alleys. Such conditions forced Hayes to resign her position [as company doctor], explaining in an interview with the *New York Times* that 'I see no point in maintaining Well Baby clinics if we are going to mix the babies' formulas with toilet water.'"

Fearing a typhoid outbreak, which was known to have happened in Iselin and other coal towns, Hayes, still employed as the company doctor, asked her employer, Shawmut Mining Co., to clean up the town and provide another source of water. When Shawmut refused, Hayes quit her job as company doctor, and 350 miners struck for nearly five months in support of her. Hanging out her shingle in Force, she took on the Shawmut Coal Company, which it turns out to have been in receivership for over 30 years, and working from her private practice, she won a decision in the US District Court for the Western District of Pennsylvania in 1945.

The path to that victory was arduous, coming only after Judge Guy K Bard from the Eastern District of Pennsylvania (headquartered in Philadelphia) was sent to Pittsburgh in 1945 to hear the case, replacing the three District judges serving the Western District who were stalling on the case. *Time Magazine* reported that Judge

Bard even "made a visit to the towns [Force and nearby Byrnedale and Hollywood] to take a look and a sniff for himself."

Ray Sprigle, Pulitzer-prize-winning investigative reporter for the *Pittsburgh Post-Gazette*, gave invaluable advice to Dr Hayes and her constituents, guiding their appeals to the FBI, to members of Congress, and to US Attorney General Tom C. Clark, a copy of that telegram being sent to President Truman. One telegram began, "We, American citizens residing in the feudal coal company towns of Force, Byrnedale, and Hollywood, appeal to you for justice" and ended with, "We the men, women, and children of the sewage-sodden towns of Shawmut Mining Co., appeal to you for action which will smash this reign of oppression and neglect and restore the American way of life to our people."

Hayes's widely reported struggle sparked an investigation by the US Department of Justice and provided the impetus for President Truman to commission the first-ever nationwide survey of sanitation, housing, and access to medical care in coal mining areas. Initiated in 1946 and published the following year by the US Department of the Interior, *A Medical Survey of the Bituminous-Coal Industry* revealed the shocking conditions of dozens of coal towns.

In 1946 the board of trustees of the Medical Society of the State of Pennsylvania unanimously commended Hayes for "her untiring and unselfish efforts," noting that the prime duty of a physician is "to guard public health" for which "pure and potable water and proper disposal of sewage" are essential.

Dr Elizabeth Hayes and Iselin's Sara L. (Hayes) Lambert were first cousins once removed. (Sara's father was Dr Elizabeth Hayes's first cousin.) But since they were almost the same age, they called each other “cousins” in their youthful days spent recreating together in and around DuBois and Force, PA.

In October 2021 journalist and author Marcia Biederman's new book titled *A Mighty Force: Dr. Elizabeth Hayes and Her War for Public Health* was published by Prometheus Books, sparking renewed interest in Elizabeth Hayes's life and work. Ms Biederman has had over 150 articles published by the *NY Times*, among other prestigious publications including *Newsday* and the *New Yorker. A Mighty Force* won a coveted place on the 2021 Mighty Women Reading List for Adults which features books about extraordinary women of the 20th century. She describes Dr Betty, as she was affectionately called by the media, as a woman who effectively became a labor leader despite having no official position in any union.

Steven Greenhouse wrote an obituary of Dr Elizabeth Hayes (1912-1984) that was published by *The New York Times* on April 1, 2022 as a part of *Overlooked*, a series of obituaries about remarkable people whose deaths, beginning in 1852, went unreported in *The Times*.

https://www.nytimes.com/2022/04/01/obituaries/elizabeth-hayes-overlooked.html

Greenhouse wrote in part, “Shawmut insisted that it couldn’t afford to build a new water system; it had declared bankruptcy four decades earlier and was still in receivership. Yet *The Pittsburgh Post-Gazette* reported that the company’s president, John D. Dickson, was taking a large salary. Judge Bard appointed two new executives to run Shawmut, ousting Dickson and his top aide. The new executives rehired Hayes and agreed to fix the sewage problems and pave the roads.”

As an aside, it is reported that Dickson's salary at Shawmut was three times the salary of General Dwight D. Eisenhower in 1945, plus a generous “expense account.”

An update at this writing from author Marcia Biederman’s website: State assembly members have introduced House Bill No. 2736 to the September 2022 Session of the General Assembly of Pennsylvania to name a stretch of Pennsylvania road the “Dr. Betty Hayes Memorial Highway.” The bill, drafted in July 2022, has been referred to the Pennsylvania House’s transportation committee. If enacted, it would be a fitting tribute to Dr Betty, who for years fought for the improvement of living conditions in north-central Pennsylvania’s Bennett’s Valley. The section of Route 255 proposed for the naming runs through the area where Dr Betty drove over unpaved roads in all kinds of weather to see her patients. She was eventually able to bring improved living conditions to the coal miners of Force, PA through her bold win over the Shawmut Coal Company in the US District Court for the Western District of Pennsylvania in 1945. The idea for the highway naming originated at a May meeting of the Elk County Board of Commissioners.

Elizabeth and Sara. Photo of Dr Elizabeth Hayes on the cover of A Mighty Force written by Marcia Biederman superimposed with a contemporaneous photo of Sara L. (Hayes) Lambert, Elizabeth's first cousin once removed.

Sara Lambert Bloom and Marcia Biederman at the DuBois Historical Society meeting when Marcia was invited to speak at a book launch in March 2022

Dr Betty Hayes

Chapter 20

Getting Back to Iselin's Public Health Journey

In Iselin this same mission fell on the strong shoulders of James P. Lambert 30 years later. His method was different from Dr Elizabeth's but by using county, state, and federal grants, starting with Operation Scarlift in the 1970s, Mr Lambert was able to rid the town of the dangerous toxic air that had hung so perniciously over Iselin for decades. And then as a member and Treasurer of the Indiana County Municipal Services Authority (ICMSA) he was given the honor of christening Iselin's now more-than-adequately-functioning Water Tank with a bottle of champagne on January 12, 1981 (which was amusing to his family and friends since he was famously a teetotaler). The plaque that was mounted on the Tank's chain link fence by the ICMSA to honor Mr Lambert upon the successful completion of his advocacy for a reliable source of clean running water for Iselin renters and owners no longer remains at the Tank, but the Water Tank continues to serve the community well. And not one to quit, with the calm determination he was known for, according to Mike Duffalo, the outstanding Executive Director of

ICMSA, and the quiet confidence he held in the promise of the Iselin Sewage Treatment Plant and installation of pipelines to the houses and churches moving forward, Mr Lambert accepted the election to a new term as Treasurer of the ICMSA that freezing January day in spite of suffering the ravages of Black Lung disease.

Nothing is more important to this narrative than to emphasize that successful completion of the mission to bring a reliable source of safe, clean running water to Iselin and to the other coal towns that had been so poorly served by R&P and the Kovalchick Water Company would not have been possible but for the visionaries who created the Indiana County Municipal Services Authority in 1973 including its first Chairman, Robert Kunkle. The leadership of Michael Duffalo, who served as its intrepid Executive Director for 46 years, was grounded in his personal history. His grandfather, Michael (Dufala) Duffalo came from Jakubany, Slovakia to nearby Ernest, PA around 1905 to work in the mines. He worked the mines at Ernest and Lucerne before becoming the Company Store Manager. Sadly, Mr Dufala was a victim of the 1918 "Spanish flu" epidemic.

He would have been very proud of his grandson Michael, who wrote: "Through ICMSA I hope I was able to contribute to the revitalization of Iselin. Jim Lambert certainly embodied the 'spirit' of the time." In his last year of service Michael was honored by the Pennsylvania Municipal Authorities Association as the 2018 Authority Employee of the Year, appropriately marking the 100th anniversary of his grandfather's passing.

Mr Lambert passed away on April 24, 1981, just three months after the Water Tank christening, so sad to be leaving but no doubt a happy man knowing that his accomplishments would make life so much more decent, more livable for his neighbors and for his beloved wife. He must have known what a big part it would play in her ability to live out her life in their Iselin home if she so chose, but neither could have imagined that would be for another 33 years.

And while he knew that it could be accomplished, he probably did not dare to predict that Iselin would have a Sewage Treatment System operational in a matter of just a year or two. He worked relentlessly and with urgency but without setting deadlines for himself and others, only missions. Failure was never an option.

Chapter 21

The Cover of This Book

Publishers are generally respectful of their authors, allowing us to bring ideas and suggestions to the design team working on the cover. Of course, the cover is a major component of successfully marketing a good history book but with all due respect to their expertise, I have asked the front cover designer of this book to consider 3 images to be used for that visual message sent to the potential reader, after asking myself what my father, James P Lambert, would have wanted on the cover.

The first image is the beautiful color photograph taken by Stan Semuskie of Iselin nestled in the rolling hills of the Appalachian Mountain chain in Western Pennsylvania. That natural beauty was a lifeline to Mr Lambert and to all of us living in the mostly harsh visual environment of a patch town.

The second, the imposing black and white vintage 1904 photograph of the Power House and Tipple (with the row of shacks known as Pigs Ear in the background) is the stark reminder of why the town of Iselin was built.

But in my heart I know that the third element to this visual composition cannot be a photo of outhouses or a photo of the smoldering boney dump or of children dirty from carefree outdoor play but with no way to wash up when the water went dry. That is not our story, it was our circumstance.

Our story is captured in a photo of the members of the Indiana County Municipal Services Authority breaking ground for Iselin's Sewage Demonstration Project along with the photo of Michael Duffalo, Executive Director of that Authority presenting a plaque to my mother, Sara L. Lambert, the widow of my father, James P. Lambert, honoring his advocacy posthumously.

Although my father was pleased with the formal photo taken of him when he was elected District Magistrate in Indiana County in 1969, with his suit and tie replacing the Sears & Roebuck work outfit he felt comfortable wearing for most of his working life, holding his best pipe that he actually had to abandon as his Black Lung disease progressed, he was too modest, too humble really to have approved of placing that photo on the cover of this book. While he derived great personal satisfaction from his role in accomplishing achievements that brought social justice to the people of Iselin, inspiration to future citizen advocates was his reward, his legacy.

And the back cover belongs to Alex Semuskie for all that he continues to do to preserve Iselin's history.

Suggested Front Cover

Village of Iselin road sign

Chapter 22

The "Big House"

"The Rosborough farm was a very big farm, very big for horsepower days. It would have been a prosperous farm as witnessed by the big house that the owners built using nothing but the best materials available and the finest craftsmen. The first house they built in the 18th century would have been of log or pit-sawn lumber, a common method of producing lumber that relied only on human power. But soon after, the big house was constructed; it remains standing today.

"A fireplace was built in every room (a total of 5)--certainly an indication of prosperity. Deeds have been traced back to 1843 but local legend and clues from its construction has it that the house was built in 1790 with a kitchen being added to the house after 1865. Prior to 1830, metals such as nails had to be brought by wagon over the mountains from the East Coast, the first beehive ovens having been opened by Cyrus in about 1830. Also, there were no cement kilns in Western Pennsylvania until the late 19th century. The bricks were made of clay and straw on site of the big house. Generally known as soft brick, they were made of a mixture of sand, clay, straw, and water put into a form which was then removed, the bricks let to dry in the sun. They never went into a kiln, thus being a sort of adobe.

"The big house was built upon a foundation of field stones about 24 inches thick. The stones are very closely fitted because there was no cement for mortar to fill the gaps. A ledge 8 to 10 inches wide was created on the inside top of the foundation on which to rest the floor joists. In a basement room the beams used for joists reveal the hickory logs flattened on 2 sides by an adz. The floorboards in the house were pit-sawn.

"Three of the 8 original walls have foundations approaching 3 feet thick; the walls are approximately 24 inches thick from foundation to the roof line. The extra thick walls were necessary to hold the fireplaces and chimneys. A huge slab of flat rock in the basement formed the bed of the hearth located in the first floor living area.

"The inside walls were then plastered in a unique way since standard plaster requires cement. They mixed clay, sand, limestone, and horsehair, wet it, and put on a ½ to ¾ inch coat called the base coat. Then a coat 1/8 to ¼ inch thick of sand, clay & more lime plus water called the "evener coat" was applied. The final or skin coat was more lime, less sand & clay, producing a smooth wall for its time.

"All the glass was float glass, spread out in forms on site. The original glass with its wavy texture remains today.

"False walls were constructed to hide the fireplaces sometime after 1865 when a coal furnace was installed in the basement providing central heat; there was a coal bin near the furnace and a chimney was built on the outside wall. Eventually the dirt floor of the basement was cemented.

"Originally there were two adjoined outbuildings, one housing the kitchen (a fire-prevention strategy) and one a washhouse, which is typical of the period. A hand pump and potbelly stove for heating the water was probably added to the washhouse after the Civil War when a kitchen was added to the big house. A coal/wood cookstove was put into the new kitchen and a new chimney added. A septic tank and leaching field was constructed sometime in the early part of the 20th century to accommodate indoor plumbing. The construction of what later became a garage probably predates the first automobile as evidenced by the big double doors on the back side of the building to accommodate hay wagons." James M. Lambert

Electricity was introduced and upgrades were made several times over the latter half of its nearly 228-year history. Some knob and tube wiring actually remained in the house but was replaced as required by the USDA when it was sold in 2018.

Sara Lambert wrote in 2008 (when she was 98 years old): "The first town manager of the Iselin was Mr Patterson whose daughters, Jean Patterson and Betty Pride, and grandchildren Jean, Donny, and Jimmy Pride we all knew. The girls grew up in this house around the beginning of the 20th century. Then came Larry Redding who married Catherine Gleason from DuBois. He got promoted to the main office and they moved to Indiana. Catherine continued to visit old friends and we got to know her. Then Mr. Douglas, who, when his children left home, moved to a smaller house in Coal Run where the mine was. When we moved in, we lived downstairs and because housing was scarce during the war, rented out three rooms upstairs and shared the bath with Ramona (Langham) and Johnny Velesig."

For over 78 years the "Big House" was home to four generations of Lamberts until it was sold by the Estate of Sara L. Lambert in 2019 to a young Iselin family.

Unsuccessful approaches had first been made to descendants of the Iselins, to Joseph Kovalchick, and to the Provost of IUP to purchase the property and donate it to a proposed non-profit Iselin Mine Museum. Given that historic late 18th-century house with its hay wagon garage and two other outbuildings in which to display large and small artifacts and its land sufficient to re-establish the Victory Garden and fruit trees, bringing back that intoxicating sight and fragrance of hillsides of blossoms each Spring, with additional land for visitor parking on a surface of "red dog," which is what the residual left when the boney dumps burned out was called, historic preservation grants could have been identified to restore the house as close to its original construction as possible and to exhibit artifacts and photographs to tell this story. An opportunity to preserve and make accessible to the public the history of this important piece of the second phase of the Industrial Revolution in America was lost.

Mrs Lambert on the porch of the Big House, c. 1990

Town of Iselin

Town of Iselin-partial view, 1958, with outhouses "down back". The one main road through town was eventually paved, becoming affectionately known as Cement Road (pronounced by locals with the accent on the first syllable) now listed as State Route 3023. Unpaved side streets acquired local eponymous names like Store Street, Barber Street, Church Street, English Street, Middle Street, and Lower Street until 911 more recently renamed them using colors, e.g. Red Street, Green Street.

Chapter 23

Not Ready To Be Called A "Ghost Town"

Coal mining was a way of life in Iselin dating back to 1903. As one miner who is the son and grandson of Iselin coal miners and who worked for 27 years 200 feet underground until his retirement in 1999 put it, "Growing up outside Indiana, all we ever knew was mining. It was a job, and the pay was pretty good. I had a bunch of nice friends and worked on good crews."

The arc of estimated populations: in 1903, 1930, 1980, and 2023= 400, 5000, 500, 150 residents in Iselin, Pennsylvania.

In the 1990s, some of Iselin's housing stock underwent updates when USDA Rural Development funds were made available as loans to "very-low-income" and grants to "elderly very-low-income" owners through the Homeownership Rehabilitation Program, designated to be used to remove health and safety hazards. But housing quality was not the critical issue by then. In 1993, a third generation Iselin coal miner who had managed to maintain his employment for decades in spite of layoffs, strikes, and finally the closings of the mines in Iselin and surrounding coal towns told the investigative reporter who interviewed him for an article he was writing for Pittsburgh's *Tribune-Review* that "80% of the people [currently living in Iselin] are at least in their 60s. Really, for the young people, there's nothing here. I'd like it to be different but that's the way it is."

The power plant in Lucerne where my father worked in the 1960s has outlasted its life expectancy and continues to be "patched up" and kept in minimal operation, burning coal to produce electricity. But Pennsylvania has the most abandoned coal mines in the U.S., making coal scarce, an increasingly expensive source of fuel. The Senate-passed infrastructure bill is giving Pennsylvania $245M to help with mitigation work "like extinguishing underground mine fires, treating water, changing out the soil, and planting grass and trees," to quote a February 2022 article in *WITF.* At this writing in early 2023, another retired third generation Iselin coal miner estimates that only a few residents of Iselin are currently employed as coal miners, commuting to nearby mines that are still in operation. But transitional work, jobs in mitigation work are on the horizon.

As I wrote in Chapter 3, I realized in the process of writing this book, "What a rich pocket of humanity we grew up in! A deep vein, as they say in R&P parlance."

And so the town lives on. One young resident of Iselin is a recent Valedictorian of his high school class and aspires to attend college to become a French teacher. He follows in the footsteps of many children who grew up in Iselin exceling in academics and going on to hold a wide range of positions in the field of education, including teachers, administrators, and coaches in K-12; faculty members at colleges and universities; a Vice Provost at a University and an Assistant Dean at a Law School; and day care staff and pre-school teachers proudly standing shoulder to shoulder with others who grew up in Iselin who went on to be employed in the trades including auto mechanics, HVAC, plumbing, carpentry, tile and bricklaying, electrical, pipe-laying, construction, small appliance repair, and more; as members of the finance, accounting, communications, and law professions; as an ophthalmologist; as nurses; as X-Ray and CT technicians, as nursing home and hospital administrators; as an ombudsman in an aging service; as cooks, food managers, and nutritionists for schools and nursing homes; as a sous chef for a large casino; as florists; as workers in cleaning services; as retail clerks and salespeople; as a VP for Customer Service of a major international corporation; as secretaries, managers, and HR directors in businesses; as the caretaker and gardener for a wealthy out of state family (who were actually friends with the NYC Iselin family); as a fine arts painter and gallery curator; as a professional photographer; as an orchestral musician; as a filmmaker; as entrepreneurs who opened businesses including restaurants and a popular food stand; as a member of the Content Team for SAT tests developed at Educational Testing Service in Princeton; as a Principle Site Reliability Engineer for Apple and others in Silicon Valley; as a member of a religious order; as manufacturing plant workers; as farmers and farmhands; as firemen and EMTs; as career military; as a DC policeman recruited to White House Secret Service, honored to have served his country by being assigned to protect several presidents successively; as an elected State Legislator; as an elected Justice of the Peace and an elected District Magistrate; as stay at home moms or dads; and yes, as coal miners or surface workers for neighboring mines.

In its heyday Iselin could claim a concentration of industrious, multi-talented, gifted people who took pride in each other's strengths and achievements; echoes of that spirit remain among the dwindling numbers of residents who are undergoing the challenging transition from having been a coal town to an uncertain future.

A daughter of a coal miner said recently, "I loved every minute of my childhood growing up in Iselin. I just wish it [living conditions] hadn't been so hard for my parents. It's sad that those hardships were not improved until 80 years after the town was built, but I'll never forget how grateful we were when it happened." Life-changing.

Yes, loyalty to Iselin runs long and deep. Alex Semuskie has collected artifacts of the mining that was done there beginning with the arrival of his grandparents from Ukraine in 1903 through his father's employment in the Iselin mines and his own through his retirement from coal mining in 1999, artifacts that had been used by generations of coal miners beginning 120 years ago. Visitors to Iselin can seek out his unique and immense private collection of memorabilia that runs the gamut from equipment to photographs to signs to documents to lunch pails. Among the items both small and massive are two old-time mining cars set on short rails. One is a half-ton car used in a low coal mine, with passages only about 4 feet high; the other is a larger ton-and-a-half car.

Hanging from the rafters in Alex's garage are miner baskets--round metal baskets with hooks on their bottoms. "Miners hung up the baskets and put belongings inside, then hung their clothing from the hooks. Most time you'd come out of the mine soaking wet."

Among the extensive lamp collection are old-time lamps that warned, rather than illuminated.

"When you had gas, the flame would go up. If the lamp would go out, there was no oxygen. They were outlawed because the open flame would ignite and cause an explosion," explains the collector.

Alex is back living in Iselin after a short stint working in construction elsewhere. This devoted collector/curator is quoted in an interview with TribLIVE in 2009, "I love the history, the remembrances of all the old people who worked in the mine and fought and died for what we have today."

Alex's brother, Stan Semuskie, has either taken or collected over 100 photographs of Iselin and its people beginning almost 120 years ago. His appreciation began at an early age when he was taking a college course at IUP, appreciation of what it means to preserve the memory of people and places and events through photography and film making so that our history is not lost in the quicksand of time.

In addition to these treasures are the stories that are still being told and retold. Viva la storytellers!

And while the streets remain unpaved, the last remaining outhouse is now retired from use.

Rolling hills of Appalachia surrounding Iselin

Alex Semuskie painted by Bill Perry

https://stan-semuskie.smugmug.com/Family/Bottleworks-gallery

"The breadth of Alex's knowledge of all aspect of mining is amazing and [during my visit] as he passed from one artifact to another, he spoke enthusiastically about its use and the time period from which it came...I chose to paint Alex holding one of the early wick lamps that was used in the mines. This lamp was called a SUNSHINE LAMP because of the particular fuel it burned." Bill Perry

Epilogue

More quoting some of Iselin's Voices, from in-person and phone interviews, texts, and emails, plus a few Adrian Iselin family anecdotes and excerpts from writings left by four who have passed away.

1. Here are two anecdotes included in the history of McIntyre, a coal town near Iselin, compiled and written in 2001 in partial fulfillment for the requirement of a Master's degree in history from Slippery Rock University of PA by Susan Ferrandiz, a descendent of McIntyre coal miners:

McIntyre, Pennsylvania, The Everyday Life Of A Coal Mining Company Town: 1910-1947 (photos, documents, memories of town residents, 2001,

http://204.235.148.201/history_of_mcintyre.htm

A letter written in 1910 to Mr Adrian Iselin, Jr from the President of a neighboring coal company based in Punxsutawney was addressed to 35 Wall Street, New York City, presumably Mr Iselin's office. That location was listed online in 2018 as a 3-bedroom, 2-bathroom apartment with an outdoor patio “in a luxury building located in the heart of the Financial District” for just over $1.1M.

Another interesting note is that in 1888 John Singer Sargent was commissioned to paint a portrait of Adrian Iselin, Jr's mother, Eleanora O'Donnell Iselin (Mrs Adrian Georg Iselin), who was born into a wealthy and prominent Baltimore family in 1821. This portrait hangs in the National Gallery of Art in Washington DC. A “premium canvas print” 14” x 24” can be purchased on Amazon for $33.

Left: Adrian Georg Iselin (1818-1905), Founder and Namesake
Right: Portrait of Mrs Adrian Georg Iselin (née Eleanora O'Donnell) (1821-1897), painted by John Singer Sargent, 1888, National Art Gallery, Washington DC

Adrian Georg Iselin, Jr (1846-1935) Mr. Iselin was a member of the New York Yacht Club, the Larchmont Yacht Club, the New Rochelle Yacht Club, earning this trophy at one of his clubs.

2. More Iselin family anecdotes from Eileen Mountjoy's "Iselin Family," part of the series *Coal Culture: People, Lives, and Stories*, Indiana University of Pennsyvania, 1981, https://www.iup.edu/library/departments/archives/coal/people-lives-stories/iselin-family.html

Adrian Jr's father, Adrian Georg Iselin (1818-1905) and his wife Eleanora (1821-1897), residents of NYC, were founding members of the Metropolitan Opera House, the American Museum of Natural History, and the Metropolitan Museum of Art. "He was a generous philanthropist to these and other organizations and died with a remaining fortune estimated at $30 million."

Neither Adrian Georg nor Adrian Jr ever lived in Pennsylvania.

"As a result of his personal interest in the area, Adrian Jr. and his family became minor celebrities in early Indiana County mining towns. Residents were more than a little awed when the elegant Iselin railroad coach pulled into their communities, and local newspapers eagerly published stories of the family's activities. On several occasions, it was noted, women and girls from the Iselin party enjoyed shopping expeditions into the various company stores." No records or memories exist of such a visit to Iselin.

Adrian Jr (b. 1846 in NYC; d. 1935 in NYC) married twice: to Louise Caylus (m. 1872; d. 1909) and to Sarah Gracie King Bronson (m. 1914; died 1931). He and Louise had four children: Adrian Iselin III, Ernest Iselin, Therese Eleanor Iselin, and Louise Marie Iselin.

3. Jane Lambert Abe, my sister, is the author of the history of Iselin's Holy Cross Church for their Golden Jubilee in 1958. Jane, the daughter of James P Lambert, Iselin's Town Manager, and his wife Sara, was a member of the choir and a leader in the Sodality at Holy Cross Church. After earning a BA from Seton Hill College in nearby Greensburg, PA, Jane was offered a position at Educational Testing Service in Princeton in 1960, writing and editing questions for their ubiquitous and powerfully influential SAT exams. Unhappy with the advantageous slant of those tests towards America's primarily white, upper classes, she left ETS to work for a time on IQ testing at the University of Iowa, eventually becoming a teacher leader in Salt Lake City's public schools. Her experience teaching gifted children there led to Jane's growing into a leadership role in professional development in gifted education across Utah and the nation. Jane was an early advocate for what Howard Gardner's pio-

neering work at Harvard became known as the Theory of Multiple Intelligences that more accurately captures the full range of abilities and talents that people possess. Jane earned advanced degrees and taught courses at the University of Utah and served as a vital member of the Board of Trustees for the McCarthey Dressman Education Foundation but before her passing in 2016, to the very end of her life she continued to push us to look beyond Gardner's original list of seven types of intelligences: visual-spatial, linguistic-verbal, logical-mathematical, bodily-kinesthetic, musical, interpersonal, and intrapersonal (to which he and his team have recently added "naturalist"). Her upbringing in Iselin no doubt was the foundation for Jane's ability to value each of these 7 intelligences, which was not the reality in American society of her time and continues to be a challenge today, although some colleges' recent decision to drop minimum SAT scores (typically required in two of the seven types listed above) as a requirement for admission is a start that she would applaud. But beyond that progress, Jane would have us remember that she saw even more room for inclusivity, more opportunity to value abilities and talents that are not yet defined or not easily measured by a test and given a numerical score that controls destinies. Jane and our sister Marie were tender and devoted caregivers to our mother in her final years, which I was able to join just in the last year, expanding my schedule of visits after my retirement.

This is the text of a *History of the Parish* written by "Miss Jane Lambert" for the booklet printed in 1958 in celebration of the Golden Jubilee of Iselin's Holy Cross Church and published in June 1958 in the *Indiana Evening Press*, re-titled "Church History." At the time she was asked by the Church to write it, Jane was a student, pursuing a BA degree at Seton Hill College in Greensburg, PA, with a double major in English and Math. It is the richest source that I have found of an Iselin "voice" who was there from the very beginning, the woman whom Jane interviewed for the piece, so here it is in its entirety. It is interesting that Jane does not name her, and I regret that I don't know the reason for that, but I find their rapport touching.

History of the Parish by Miss Jane Lambert

It was a hard life those people led. Most of them had just come to America, and they had to get used to a new town and a new language and a new country all at the same time. "The R and P started building houses around the turn of the century," the oldtimer remembered, "and many of the people lived in these new homes. Some of them still lived in the tarpaper shacks down by the coal tipple, though—they called it the Pig's Ear. It was in one of those shacks that the first Mass was said. What's that letter you have, there?"

I showed her the letter, dated August 23, 1904, that I had obtained at the chancery in my search of the history of Holy Cross parish.

"Oh, Mrs. White was the one who wrote to the Bishop!" she exclaimed. "So that's how it got started. Let's see. She asks that a priest be sent out to care for '75 Italian people, 30 Poles, and a few English' who lived here. I don't remember the priest's name, but I remember that those ladies cleaned out one of the shacks, and he set up his altar there. It wasn't very nice or pleasant, but that was what we used until they were able to move our 'church' into one of the houses. We were a mission from Indiana then, and Father McNelis was our pastor. The priest would come out to Iselin on Saturday night and stay over for mass the next day at old Pat Carroll's house—right up here at 111 English Street. Oh, you have another letter there."

I showed her the letter I had which Father McNelis received on March 24, 1905, from Lucius W. Robinson, then president of the Rochester and Pittsburgh Coal and Iron Company. In it he indicated the company's intention of cooperating with the people in building a church.

"Yes," she said, "we started building our church very soon after that. I remember that while we were building it, we had our first ice cream festival. We didn't know how much ice cream to order, so we guessed at 25 gallons—it was all gone by seven o'clock! Everybody came that day from miles around. It was quite a success!"

I mentioned that the first record of the parish that the chancery had was a financial report written in September, 1908.

"Oh yes, I remember. Father Francis Wieczorek was our first pastor. He lived in a house down on Barber Street. Times were still hard for the people then. The mines were booming, and the new houses were built, but these people had to get used to the new town—and many of them to a new country and a new language. The church wasn't exactly poor, but it was far from being wealthy. We had an old parlor organ in the church at first, but it didn't last long. In fact, it wasn't long at all till it just fell apart—old age, I guess—and we were looking for a new one. The Nyerges family came to our rescue, but this organ wasn't too much better. You had to pick up the keys each time you pressed them before they would play again! We had a violinist here one time for confirmation and it was quite embarrassing. He played Gounod's 'Ave Maria' with the organ accompaniment, but he was way ahead of the organist for the whole song—he didn't wait for her to pick up the keys!

"The rectory was built sometime in these next few years; I don't remember exactly what year, but Father Anthony Baron was the first priest to live in it. He came in 1911, didn't he? Yes, and right after he left, the rectory burned down. I can't remember what year, but the house burned in January and the church burned in April—either that year or the year after. It was during Lent that the church caught fire, I remember, and we had services that night! Some of the people thought that the altar boys had been careless and they always blamed the fire on them. I guess we'll never know.

"Well, anyway, the fire started an hour or so after services were over; we had been having a party for one of the boys who was leaving that week for the Army, when someone burst in, shouting that the church was on fire. You never saw anyone move so fast as we did that night. It couldn't have taken more than two minutes for all of us to get there! I'll never forget the sight of Father Zmijewski running up the hill, wringing his hands and worrying about the Blessed Sacrament! We found out later that one of the men had got it out, but he was worried for a while.

"Mass was said in the old town hall until the new church was built. I don't know when that was; it couldn't have been too much later, though; we started as soon as we could."

I told her that the Bishop had a record of the permission granted on August 6, 1918, to spend $13,000 to build a church and a rectory.

She thought this over for a minute. "That sounds right. We had the church finished before Father Forysiak moved in. Was that

1922? Yes, August, 1922. Those were the years—the Roaring Twenties! Father Gawronski came in 1925; his term was longer than that of any of our other pastors—almost fifteen years. He must have had a rough time of it, watching over his flock during those depression years.

"Father Kuklecki came to us in September of 1939, and his was quite a busy term. He started right in that year organizing the Christian Mothers and the Sodality. I don't remember if they were started before that or not, but at any rate, it was about then that they became active. He began the custom of services for the Poor Souls at the cemetery each November and taught the parishioners much respect for it. The grotto was built around that time by some of the men from the parish, and the outdoor statue was donated by a lady from Hayes, Pennsylvania in appreciation for Father's help in some matter. Oh, there were so many things accomplished during those war years! During the long winter evenings there were ping-pong and boxing and all sorts of games in the church basement for all the kids. In 1944 a big wooden cross was donated by the R. and P. for the cemetery. Also in the spring of 1944, the big front porch of the rectory was closed in and transformed into an office, and it was right after that that Father was transferred.

"In June, 1944, Father Iwaniski came. It was he who, noticing the need of the parishioners in the two mission churches, St. Gertrude's in McIntyre and St. Anthony's in Aultman, asked for an assistant. Until then the priest had celebrated one Sunday mass in Iselin and one in either McIntyre or Aultman, alternating each week between the two churches. Those families who didn't have a car or friends with a car had to be satisfied with Mass only every other week. When Father Shinar came in March, 1945, the schedule was straightened out.

"Then, in early 1947, the people of McIntyre asked the Bishop if they might become a parish. On March 8 the petition was granted, St Gertrude's Church became a parish, and St. Anthony's was made a mission from McIntyre. Father Stanley was our pastor then, and he remembers yet how our people, in their concern about their ability to finance a church, united and cooperated with him to such an extent that our parish grew and prospered, despite the decline in population of the town.

"After the parish was split, we didn't need an assistant and Father Shinar was transferred. We hated to see him go—he had done a lot of good work for us. The Sodality worked very hard with him; they produced a few plays and even instituted a library in the basement of the church. I think it was Father Shinar, too, who organized the St. John Bosco Society here for the grade school boys.

"It was during that time that the mortgage was burned. There had been a $4500 mortgage held on the church by the coal company ever since it was built in 1918. Father Stanley asked the board of directors of the R and P what could be done about it; they very generously offered to cancel it. We really celebrated then—we had a big party, and all the officials came and helped us to burn the mortgage.

"In February, 1949, Father Noroski became our pastor. Such a good man—and a wonderful priest, too. The organizations were never so active and so vital as they were during his time. It seemed as though he provided an individual inspiration for each parishioner. While he was here, Father was appointed Diocesan Director of

Sodalities, and he began the immense task of organizing the union of sodalities in the diocese.

"Father Borkowski started off his term here with a bang by organizing a campaign for a new organ. In a little more than a year, the new organ was dedicated on October 24, 1954. Father did a lot of work with the young people of the parish; he organized a county girls softball league and entered in it Holy Cross Church's sodality team. Every year, all the grade school kids would go up to the church on Sunday in early spring and sign up for their teams in the two softball leagues—one for the boys and one for the girls. And when he left in June, 1957, he left behind a beautifully decorated basement, with a brand new floor, tiled walls, and, down at one end, a modern, efficient kitchen.

"Father Rendziniak succeeded him, but it wasn't very long until he was replaced by Father Pirulli. My goodness! Here we are at June, 1958, already! That was quite a journey in the past!"

"It certainly was," I said as I closed my notebook; "Iselin is quite a town!"

4. Here is the letter from Jane (Mrs Daniel T.) Heyer that was also included in the booklet printed by Holy Cross Church in celebration of their Golden Jubilee in 1958. It was sent from her address on April 19, 1958: 41 Crestline Ave., Bethpage, L.I.N.Y.

Dear Father Pirulli:

Your kind invitation to attend the Golden Anniversary of Holy Cross Church on June 8, 1958 was received and it is with great disappointment that I will be unable to attend in person, but will be with you all in spirit. One of my granddaughters is being married on June 8th, otherwise I would be at your Golden Jubilee Celebration.

On June 8, 1909 I was married in Holy Cross Church and if my husband were still alive, would be celebrating my 49th Anniversary. Two of my nine children were born in Iselin and baptized in Holy Cross Church.

Personally, I have many pleasant memories of the time spent in Iselin and many sad ones. With fond memories I think back of the days when my mother and myself washed and ironed Altar linens, fixed the Altars and even enjoyed ourselves sweeping and scrubbing the floors as we knew we were working for our Church. My sister, Margaret and myself taught the children Catechism, sometimes with the assistance of a Priest and at other times alone. In those days the Priest had to travel from Indiana via "horse and buggy" and with the dirt roads, inclement weather etc. it was quite a hardship. Father Paroline was the Priest to say the first Mass in Iselin. (I am forwarding you a picture of him, in case you did not obtain one as I believe there were few in existence. Whether or not you use this picture, I would appreciate your mailing it back to me.)

Mass was said in a shanty across from the Coal Tipple, known then as the "Pig's Ear." My Father, Patrick Carroll and James Patterson obtained it from the Company [R&P] and they along with other good men of Iselin did a thorough job of "face lifting." Mr. William Hazelett, a carpenter, made a table which was used for the Altar and wooden benches for the parishioners which consisted of one to two dozen persons. Shortly afterwards, Mr. Hazelett was called to his Final Reward, due to an accident in the mines. It wasn't long after this we started negotiations to build our Church. Fund raising was the important agenda. I shall never forget our first Ice Cream Festival. I asked Father McNeales for permission; he was rather skeptical and said I would have to do it on my own. From my efforts, I realized a profit of $25.00. Father was very pleased and I undertook a second one. From then on the men of the Parish took over and it became quite a social and prosperous affair.

Rose Patterson Dowdell was our first organist. My brothers, Patrick and Joseph Carroll were the first altar boys. A family by the name of McConville moved to Iselin; their son Robert became a very faithful altar boy. He had to go to work at a young age and lost a limb, due to an accident in the mines. Bernard Lebondosky, another faithful altar boy, because of his father's death had to work at an early age; shortly afterwards God called him to his Eternal Reward, the result of a mine accident. These two boys were in my Catechism class and excellent students and both my right hand when I wanted work done around the Church. During my time in Iselin, my dear mother also passed away, so you see my memories are of a mixture.

I humbly apologize for taking up your time with this long letter, but thought I might be able to give you a few notes of interest. It is so wonderful for members of a Parish to work and watch it grow; it must be edifying for a Pastor like yourself to be inspired to a celebration of this kind. I can wish you no greater wish than your future be as happy and prosperous as your past. I wish each and every one of you a very Happy and Blessed Day.

Enclosed you will find a check for $10.00 as my contribution. It is with regret that circumstances prevent me from sending you a more substantial donation.

I am looking forward to receiving the program booklet and am sure it will be a great success. Please remember me and my family in your prayers. Sincerely, Jane (Mrs. Daniel T.) Heyer

And she added: Yes I might add my parents are responsible for a Catholic Church in Iselin. Mary Ann & Patrick Carroll.

This lovely woman was a founding member of the Holy Cross Church parish, doing many things including washing and ironing the altar linens, sweeping and scrubbing floors, teaching catechism, raising money, and mourning those lost in mine accidents-- a true and righteous pillar of the early Iselin community.

5. I enjoyed learning these stories about three generations of Durands during my phone interviews with Ruth Durand Shields and her aunt, Minerva (Herky) Durand Balcome (1923-). Herky is the nickname she earned as a child by being as strong as Hercules, or perhaps in her case it was "strong-willed"! She is the daughter of David and Josephine Durand who moved their family from Somerset, PA in 1937 when David established his work as a coal miner in Iselin. They lived for a time at the Iselin Hotel before moving into a double housing unit; the couple had 11 children. Herk's family became devoted members of Iselin Union Church. Her mother Josephine also served as Head of the PTA, all of Josephine and David's children having attended Iselin Elementary School and Elders Ridge High School. Herky graduated from ERHS in 1941. As a young man, Clifford, one of Herky's brothers, worked in the Civil Conservation Corp, established in 1933 by FDR. "Under the guidance of the Departments of the Interior and Agriculture, CCC employees fought forest fires, planted trees, cleared and maintained

access roads, re-seeded grazing lands and implemented soil-erosion controls." Ruth, the daughter of Clifford Durand and Roberta Bowser, was born and raised in Iselin. She remembers that her father told stories of having planted trees in Cook Forest State Park, which now advertises: "'The Best Old-Growth Forest' in America, Cook Forest, PA is home to some of the tallest trees in northeastern U.S.," some of them probably having been planted by her father. Clifford was a devoted leader of the congregation of Iselin Union Church. No doubt drawing on his period serving in the CCC, Clifford also faithfully managed the Iselin Union Cemetery from 1960 until his passing in 2004. Ruth remembers that her father mowed the entire Cemetery (pre-riding mower) and dug graves by hand even as he suffered from Black Lung disease, as did her grandfather David. Ruth married Terry Shields, whose family owns V. C. Shields & Sons, a business in Indiana. In 1956 it was this company that converted Iselin's electrical system to 60 hz. (See http://electrical-science.blogspot.com/2009/12/history-of-power-frequency.html?m=1)

I was honored to interview Herky, at age 99 being the oldest Iselin resident interviewed for this narrative. She was delighted to contribute her memories and was very touched to let us know that many, many members of the Durand family are buried in Iselin Union Cemetery, which she last visited during her pilgrimage home to celebrate her 90th birthday.

6. I learned more fascinating stories during my phone interviews with Mary Menotti Abbati (1928-). Both she and her younger brother Louis were born in an upstairs bedroom of a double house at #55 Lower Street, which burned down shortly after the family left

Iselin in 1952. Mary and Louis were raised in Iselin, the daughter and son of Leone Menotti, an Iselin coal miner, and his wife Carolina Armani Menotti. Mary married a native of Iselin, Angelo Abbati who was the son of a coal miner Joseph Abbati, an émigré from Italy who came to work the mines, and his wife Pearl. While Joseph and Pearl lived and died in Iselin, Mary and Angelo lived in Iselin only until Angelo worked his way to several jobs in retail (none allowed to be within the town limits of Iselin, which was prohibited by the town's owner as competition to the Company Store), eventually accepting the position as caretaker and gardener of the private estate of a successful businessman in Michigan, a position he held for 48 years. Angelo's employers were devoted to the Abbati family and loved that Angelo could "fix anything" and "make anything grow," true to the talent and spirit of Iselin men. Members of his employer's family, who were actually friends with the NYC Iselin family, continue a lifelong friendship to this day with the Abbatis. Mary's early life in Iselin was challenging since she became the caretaker of her father and younger brother following the early death of her mother from TB, her duties actually requiring her to drop out of school at age 14. Texaco began its sponsorship of *Live from the Metropolitan Opera* in December 1940 and one of Mary's fondest memories as a teenager in the 1940s is sitting in the living room of their family home in Iselin (alone) listening to the radio broadcast every Saturday afternoon. She can still hear the famous voice of Milton Cross, the host, and the voices of the many world-renowned singers she heard performing what became some of her favorite operas. Later in life Mary was caretaker of her father in Michigan as he suffered and eventually succumbed to the ravages of Black Lung Disease. Before her husband's passing, Mary and Angelo made more than 12 trips to visit Angelo's ancestral home in the Umbria region of Italy and surrounding countries (whose boundaries were frequently changing as political battles raged on), even visiting Cepletischis, the hometown of Angelo's mother Pearl. One of Mary and Angelo's five children, Joseph, is an artist and a Curator at a Gallery in San Francisco. (See https://josephabbati.art)

Mary's mother-and father-in-law, Joseph and Pearl Abbati are buried in the Iselin Union Cemetery along with Mary's brother Louis Menotti and Mary and Angelo's baby daughter Analita Abbati, who died in infancy.

I was honored to interview Mary, a second member of that treasured older generation of Iselin residents.

The Menotti home, a single house at #55 Lower Street where both Mary and her brother Louis were literally born and raised

Mary Menotti in her teens with her dog Lucky, the outhouse in the background not at all detracting from the glamor shot. Check out the Pompadour hairstyle!

Louis Menotti with his sister Mary and her husband Angelo Abbati. That's a clothesline pole in the background.

Mary and Angelo Abbati in their Iselin living room. Plastic curtains were popular during WWII.

The Abbati and Menotti graves in the Iselin Union Cemetery: Angelo's parents Joseph and Pearl Abbati who were emigres from Italy; Analita, infant daughter of Mary and Angelo Abbati, and Louis Menotti.

Louis Menotti (with the mustache) and his "Iselin gang of friends," taken when Lou came back to Iselin to attend one of the Memorial Day gatherings that the Iselin Union Cemetery Association sponsored. He loved their reunion, spending the day with old friends, telling stories. Lou died just a few months later. His children and grandchildren traveled to Iselin to follow Lou's wishes to have his ashes buried with full Military Honors in a grave that Alex Semuskie prepared for his Iselin buddy, as he did for so many.

7. Wonderful stories were entrusted to me during my phone interviews with Dorothy Knopick Parchinsky (1933-) who was raised in Iselin, honoring my work as the author of *Iselin* with her recollections. She is the daughter of Anna and William Knopick; her father worked in the Iselin mines for 48 years. Dorothy was a member of the Senior Sodality and a devoted member of the choir at Holy Cross Church in which she sang until the age of 29 when she left Iselin to marry Andrew Parchinsky, a member of the U.

S. Air Force. Dorothy is the oldest of five children; her youngest sister Jean continues to live in the family home in Iselin and Dorothy travels often from her home in Ohio to visit, planning to move back to Iselin to be with family and friends since her husband has passed away. When her family was able to purchase both sides of the double house in which they lived in Iselin, her parents generously welcomed Gilda Maruschek to remain their tenant in the other side. Only after Gilda passed away did they break through and expand the Knopick family home, installing a spacious bathroom. Dorothy, whose nickname was Dottie although she prefers to be called Dorothy in her adult years, credits her musicality to her father William, who played the violin in his youth. She and her sisters Eileen, Evelyn, and Jean are proud of their only brother, William Jr who served as a policeman in Washington D.C. before being recruited to the Secret Service, in which he served for 35 years. Many Iselin residents were thrilled when Bill generously hosted their visits to DC, taking them on private tours of the White House.

Along with those of Herky and Mary, Dorothy's memories add immeasurably to the details that contribute towards the goal of having this book earn its title, "A Rich History of a Western Pennsylvania Coal Town in Appalachia."

8. I learned innumerable and invaluable details through my phone interviews with Alex (middle name Thomas, which he never uses) Semuskie, who was raised in Iselin and remains a lifelong resident. Alex is a third generation Iselin coal miner, son of Alex Semuskie, a second generation Iselin coal miner, and his wife Edith. In his youth he served as an altar boy at Holy Cross Church. Alex is an active member of the Iselin Union Cemetery Association, and is much appreciated for creating the brick structures for the Cemetery's Memorials and for preparing the earth for the placement of new headstones. Because of his extensive knowledge of all things Iselin, Alex has frequently been interviewed by various historical and media organizations. He maintains an immense collection of coal mining memorabilia which he keeps in a series of garage-like buildings near his home that can perhaps one day become the Iselin Mine Museum with non-profit status, given some thoughtful fund-raising efforts going forward. But for now, he just loves "mining" the past and receiving curious visitors to his collection informally. "I like going back in time," Alex said in an interview for the *Tribune Review*. "Even as a kid, I was always a pack rat. I saved everything I ever had." When it comes to mining artifacts, Alex says, "I have almost everything there is to have." And that even includes a large wooden sculpture of a miner that his wife had a chainsaw sculptor make!

To learn more about the awesome painting of Alex and its creator, the fine arts painter named Bill Perry, go to the website set up by his brother Stan:

https://stan-semuskie.smugmug.com/Family/Bottle-works-gallery

Comparing Alex to all the renowned collectors of mining artifacts in America, Bill writes, "The breadth of Alex's knowledge of all aspects of mining is amazing and [during my visit] as he passed from one artifact to another, he spoke enthusiastically about its use and the time period from which it came...I chose to paint Alex holding one of the early wick lamps that was used in the mines. This lamp was called a SUNSHINE LAMP because of the particular fuel it burned.”

Semuskie mines the past

The Smithton man collects mine artifacts ranging from carbide lamps to coal cars.

By SANDRA FISCHIONE DONOVAN
For the Tribune-Review

Outside a pair of garages on this Indiana County property, it's wintry cold, but a coal stove warms the air inside.

Coal was once more than a way to heat the garages. For Alex Semuskie, 56, coal was a way of life. For 27 years, until his 1995 retirement, he worked 200 feet underground, mining the fuel deep inside mines.

"Now I work 200 feet in the air," says Semuskie, who works in construction.

Semuskie's home in Smithton has many coal-mining artifacts. But in the coal-heated garages near his parents' home outside Indiana, he has stored many more collectibles: carbide lamps, photographs, signs, helmets and even mining cars.

"I like going back in time," Semuskie says. "Even as a kid, I was always a pack rat. I saved everything I ever had."

When it comes to mining equipment examples, Semuskie said, "I have most everything there is to have."

(See MINES, Page 2A)

Alex Semuskie, of Smithton, wears a soft miner's helmet from his collection of mining artifacts.

Coal-mining artifacts stoke collector's enthusiasm

Seeking collectors

Top: Alex

Bottom: Collector of Artifacts

9. I was honored to receive important pieces of information for this book from texts and a phone interview with Debra Semuskie, who was raised in Iselin and remains a lifelong resident. Debbie is the daughter of Curtis Askins and his wife Helen and daughter-in-law of Alex Semuskie and his wife Edith; both Curtis and Alex were Iselin coal miners. After her father passed away in 1980, her mother lived another 30 years, which is often the story of widows of coal miners. Debbie invited Helen to live with her and her husband, Tim Semuskie for two years before Helen eventually needed a skilled nursing facility in her final period. Iselin people take care of their own. Debbie was so kind and responsive when I asked her (from my home here in Maine, over 600 miles away) to literally run all over town and take cellphone photos of the Veteran's Monument and the 1994 Iselin Marsh Pond Replacement Project. And she tried her best to find that plaque honoring my father, James P. Lambert that was removed when the chain link fence around the Iselin Water Tower was painted in recent years. Gone but not forgotten, since we found the newspaper articles from the dedication on January 12, 1981, with photographs of that frigid but glorious day for Iselin.

10. I was able to put together more of the mosaic of the story of Iselin from information I received through correspondence and a phone interview with Catherine Steffenino Miller, daughter of Jack and Beatrice Steffenino. Although she and her immediate family were never residents of Iselin, currently Catherine serves as the Treasurer of the Iselin Union Cemetery Association's Board of Directors, now working to create the plaque for all those who rest in unmarked graves, including some miners. A graduate of the Uni-

versity of Pittsburgh, her father Jack was a popular English teacher at Elders Ridge High School and then served as the School's much respected Principal. My siblings and I were fortunate enough to have had Mr Steffenino as our English teacher at ERHS. I remember well that list of vocabulary words we were tested on, expected to know the spelling, the meaning, and the pronunciation of 100 new words each week. (And I am hoping and praying that he would be proud of my writing in this book!) Catherine's father's sisters, her aunts Anna Michelotti and Alma Gasperino and their families were much beloved residents of Iselin, respectively a teacher and a grocer (at the "Y" with her husband Henry—which was allowed by R&P since their "mom and pop" store was located just outside the town limits of Iselin). In addition to providing leadership as an educator, Mr Steffenino was also a valuable and admired civic leader. He is pictured in a photo in Chapter 16 along with other members of the Indiana Country Municipal Authority Association, published on January 12, 1981 in the Indiana Gazette to mark the ribbon-cutting ceremonies to celebrate the Water Renovation project in Lucerne, Jacksonville, and Iselin. Their smiles certainly reflect the joy they felt in achieving this life-changing gift to the families of these coal towns.

11. Wonderful recollections surfaced in emails and phone interviews with Andrea Jean Ploskunak Hallman, my next-door neighbor in Iselin and childhood playmate. She is the daughter of Andrew Ploskunak, Iselin coal miner, and his wife Josephine, and her personal memories are sprinkled throughout the book. I'm so very grateful that she was able to send me a copy of the *Golden*

Jubilee booklet from Holy Cross Church that she retrieved from her mountain of Iselin memorabilia. Andrea Jean also shared with me that neither of her parents ever owned a car but rather than relying exclusively on the Company Store, she remembers her father taking them to Indiana to purchase school clothes in the Fall, riding the Lanich bus that stopped twice a day in Iselin on its run to Indiana. Her father also made purchases from a merchant who came to Iselin periodically in the 1950s with his van full of merchandise for sale, much like the horse and wagon merchants of the 19th century. His inventory included pots and pans, carpets, and other household items; he would also take orders for specific items, such as the one bicycle that her father purchased for her and her three siblings to share. Her father was able to work around the prohibition of retail stores in Iselin to provide good things for his family at affordable prices. After graduating from Elders Ridge High School, Andrea Jean passed the Civil Service exam and had dreams of moving to Washington DC to accept a position there. Instead, she took a position with a firm in Indiana where she worked her way up to an HR management position. She purchased a car and got her license (in that order!) and began a routine that she sustained for many years, driving weekly to Iselin to take her mother shopping and to take her father, when he was suffering from both Black Lung and Parkinson's disease, and subsequently her mother to their doctors' appointments. Her parents appreciated her devoted caretaking, loving and reliable, and often expressed to Andrea Jean their gratitude. She continues to visit the Iselin Union Cemetery to tend their graves.

Andrea Jean Ploskunak admiring her father Andrew's famous gladiolas

Andrea Jean (seated) with Sally Steffenino, daughter of Harry and Helen and niece of Jack Steffenino. None of the members of the Steffenino family ever lived in Iselin but obviously had built friendships there. Jack is shown with the members of the ICMSA in the 1981 photo in Chapter 16; his devotion to his "flock" as a civic leader and educator is captured by his daughter Catherine Steffenino Miller's narrative in Epilogue #10.

Dianna Lynn Ploskunak and the granddaughter of Iselin neighbors Gilda and Joe Maruschak in front of a row of outhouses and coal bins, with another duplex seen in the distance across the alley, their outhouses and coal bins located just behind those seen in this photo.

Josephine Ploskunak holding Andrea Jean, the first of her 4 children. Over her left shoulder is the shed on Cement Road where the miners were picked up and dropped off to commute to neighboring mines.

Andrea Jean

12. I received a treasure of information through emails and my in-person interview with Diana Heard Suman—things that I had never known although our families were lifelong friends. Diana's paternal grandfather, Thomas Charles Heard, was born in Bristol, England. TC married Lula Florence Henry from Clarion County, PA and TC's work as a coal miner began in Whiskey Run, PA where Diana's father, William Isaac Heard was born in 1909. To escape the notoriously rough and rowdy times in Whiskey Run, TC moved his family when William (Bill) was a boy, re-establishing his work as a coal miner just 5 miles away, in the town of Iselin. When TC was made Face Boss by the R&P Coal Company, the family moved to a single house on English Street in Iselin. To help his son clearly understand his options going forward, during the summer after 8th grade, Bill's last year attending Iselin Elementary School, TC had

Bill work in the mine. Diana explained, “TC secretly asked his crew to put Bill in the lowest part of the mine where the ceiling was very low. At the end of the summer, TC asked Bill to decide if he was going to carry a coal miner's lunch box or a bunch of books. He chose the books and a paper bag lunch.” After graduating from Elders Ridge Vocational School and earning a degree in 1932 from Indiana Teachers College (which later became Indiana University of Pennsylvania), Bill continued to live in Iselin with his parents, commuting to teach elementary school in the neighboring coal mining towns of Coal Run and McIntyre as well as in the Iselin Elementary School and then continuing to commute from Iselin to teach at the Elders Ridge High School beginning in 1933, where he taught Chemistry for 30 years. Bill met Ann Rabico (originally Anastasia Rabickow), who was teaching in West Lebanon at the time, at a teachers' “meet & greet” in 1933. Married women were not permitted to teach at this time in Pennsylvania so after dating, they eloped to west Virginia and were married in secret in 1936 so that Ann could continue teaching. In 1938 Ann resigned from teaching, and their son Thomas was born in the Iselin home that she and Bill shared with Bill’s parents, TC and Lula Heard. Soon after, Bill moved his family to Elders Ridge where their second child, Diana (born in Indiana County Hospital) joined the family, eventually purchasing a lovely brick house (with a good well and indoor plumbing) in Elders Ridge. Both Thomas and Diana attended Iselin Elementary School, during WWII Tom choosing to live with his grandparents in Iselin during the school week and Diana choosing to be bused from Elders Ridge for the years she was enrolled there. Both Tom (1938-2008) and Diana became teachers, and their mother, Ann, went back to teaching during WWII, allowed to teach since most men were at war. Diana went on to a career teaching math at Redbank Valley and at Apollo Ridge Middle School. At his all too early passing her brother, Thomas Charles Heard III, was Professor Emeritus at Edinboro State College where he taught physics, after having started his teaching career by replacing his father for a year at Elders Ridge High School while Bill was at West Virginia University on a scientific grant. Ann taught for a short time at Iselin Elementary School; during the final decades of her teaching career, she taught at Sunnyside Elementary School in nearby Spring Church, along with her Iselin friend Sara Lambert who was also hired to go back to teaching, even though she was a married woman with five children. Upon his retirement from Elders Ridge High School, Bill Heard accepted a position in the Dept of Chemistry at IUP where he taught for 12 years while he continued to live in Elders Ridge, awarded the title of Professor Emeritus upon his second retirement, this time from IUP, in 1974. Upon his passing in 1977 he was honored at IUP with the establishment of the William Heard Memorial Scholarship. Several of my siblings and I were privileged to have studied Chemistry with Mr Heard and I also took Physics with his son Tom at Elders Ridge High School.

13. Substantial contributions to this book were made through written and phone conversations with my sister, Marie Lambert McGee (1939-) and written information from my brother, the late James Michael Lambert (1941-2020). We are three of the five children raised in Iselin, daughters and son of James P. Lambert, Town Manager of Iselin, and his wife Sara.

In her youth, Marie was a member of the choir, a leader in the Sodality, and a volunteer in the office of Holy Cross Church, typing and duplicating the weekly bulletin. A graduate of Elders Ridge High School, Marie earned her BS in Business Education (minor in English) at Indiana State College (now Indiana University of Pennsylvania) and her MBA from Plymouth (NH) State College (now Plymouth State University). Marie is a Teacher/Consultant in Accounting and Finance with approximately ten years' experience as a certified public accountant, specializing in healthcare finance; she is widely admired for her over twenty years volunteering in non-profit organizations. She retired in 2001 from BerryDunn, Certified Public Accountants and Management Consultants, headquartered in Portland, ME. Prior to that Marie was with Smith, Bachelder & Rugg, Certified Public Accountants, headquartered in Lebanon, NH. She held a tenured position teaching at Colby-Sawyer College in New London, NH and also taught accounting in the MBA program at the International University of Japan in Urasa. Niigata Prefecture, Japan. A member of the Healthcare Financial Management Association since 1993, Marie continues to be active in the Northern New England Chapter to this day. HFMA is a professional membership association with more than 83,000 members who share an interest in the financial management of the delivery of healthcare services. There are over 60 chapters in the US. Marie served in the various officer roles of the Chapter and of the Region, became a Fellow of HFMA in 1998 and received the HFMA Medal of Honor in 2007. In addition to her very active professional life, she is a family anchor as daughter and sister, wife and mother, and now grandmother and great grandmother.

Marie is the family's historian; she released a 127-page book with 96 photographs, some in black and white and some in color, in December 2022 titled *And We'll All Go Together—An Irish Family Emigrates to America* which she co-authored with one of our 25 Lambert first cousins, Michael Patrick Lambert II (IBSN-13: 978-0-578-27670-0). Their book is stunningly beautiful, the cover an acrylic painting by Marie's artist daughter Elizabeth McGee from a photograph that Marie took on her visit to County Clare, Ireland in 2019. The title is a line from *Wild Mountain Thyme,* a traditional Irish folk song. In the book the Lambert family history is traced back to 1795 in Ireland; a map of Ireland/Wales/England is included in the book as a helpful visual guide to their journey, many coming to America via England where they learned coal mining skills after famine and brutal British rule made tenant farming and fishing untenable occupations in their beloved Ireland. Even a color photograph of the Lambert Coat of Arms is included! A history of the Hayes family, our maternal line, will be Marie's next publication.

In her childhood, Marie was the peacemaker and cheerleader in the family, bringing her sense of joy to the Lambert home by encouraging all of us in our endeavors. She enjoyed doing creative things like annually painting the nativity scene on the front door window and Frosty on the side door window at Christmas time. Marie and our older sister Jane (1938-2016) were tender and devoted caregivers to our mother in her final years.

14. In addition to the extensive essay, "The Construction of the Rosborough Farmhouse" that our brother, James M. Lambert (1941-2020), wrote for inclusion in *WPML Seller Disclosure State-*

ment Attachment A, which is the document that Marie wrote as the Administrator for the Estate of Sara L. Lambert, James also wrote a letter to our sister Jane in 2008. In it was additional information on the construction of the "Big House." Excerpts from both, along with comments from Jane and our mother, Sara L. Lambert, about the house, have been quoted in Chapter 22.

Jim also wrote of being instructed by his father on how to dig a hole a safe distance from the "Big House" in the 1950s for the family's new septic tank, a replacement for the old "French cesspool" which was proving to be inadequate as usage increased with our growing family. The cesspool was also found to be draining into the well, polluting the original source of water for the house. Jim also dug new trenches for leaching, which he did with an Iselin buddy. He was 12 years old.

Jim was employed by West Penn Power and also served as the chief safety manager at Canterbury Coal, Indiana County until the Company went non-union in 1985. In 2000, Canterbury Coal was listed as the ninth largest underground mining company in Pennsylvania.

In his youth, Jim served as an altar boy at Iselin's Holy Cross Church. He was a devoted son and brother, a proud father of his four children, and a loving grandfather and great grandfather. A great storyteller himself, Jim also was a repository of many a family story he heard as he fished the streams with his father and uncles or worked with them on building projects in the Big House and Camp Shamrock.

15. Information found on their website: Indiana County Municipal Services Authority

http://icomsa.org/About-Us/ICMSA-About-Us

Michael Duffalo is the much-respected Executive Director of the ICMSA from its inception in 1973 until his retirement in 2019. He and his wife Anita continue to live in retirement near Iselin and to keep in touch with many of the thousands of people he worked with in coal towns throughout Indiana County, working through complex issues to bring relief to them. He kindly provided a copy of the article featured in Chapter 16 written by Carl Kologie in January 1981 for the *Indiana Evening Press*; it is one of the most important contributions to this narrative. Michael wrote to the author of this book: "You should be applauded for capturing the culture and spirit of Iselin, the mining boom, and the visions of your father. You have so eloquently captured an important keepsake of our heritage." He should be applauded for his heroic work.

16. Nostalgic memories bubbled to the surface in my phone interviews with Tim Semuskie, who was raised in Iselin and remains a lifelong resident, son of Alex Semuskie, a second generation Iselin coal miner, and his wife Edith, who was my mother's best friend in Iselin. As a youngster Tim served as an altar boy at Holy Cross Church. Tim and his father were hired by my mother in the 1980s, after my father's passing, to do some much-needed updates to the "Big House." I especially loved how they wallpapered and painted in a stunning early American style what was the bedroom for us three girls in our youth. It then became the favorite guest room for when we returned with our families for visits and the favorite

guest room for the many visitors my mother hosted. She called it the "Rose Room." Tim's good heart is evident in his years of caring for his aging parents and in-laws before their passing.

17. I was blessed with receiving emails and having phone conversations with Stan Semuskie, who was raised in Iselin, son of Alex Semuskie, Iselin coal miner, and his wife Edith and brother of Alex and Tim and Greg. In his youth, Stan served as an altar boy at Holy Cross Church. He began taking photographs of Iselin--the people, the town, the mines--for a Photo Journalism Essay required by a course he took while enrolled at IUP in 1974. That interest led Stan to taking or gathering over 200,000 photos. He used several thousand of these to create a professional website, over 100 of which are of Iselin subjects, some that he took and others that he gathered from as long ago as 1903:

https://stan-semuskie.smugmug.com/Photo-Restorations/Iselin-Pennsylvania

This book has been blessed with Stan's having given permission to include many of the photographs from his various portfolios. His generosity reflects Stan's love of our humble little hometown, his love for his family, and his lasting connection to his Iselin friends and neighbors. Our parents must be beaming!

Before his retirement Stan traveled the world to pursue assignments in the various positions he held in Customer Service in the Semiconductor Industry: Engineer, Manager, Director. His last position was Vice President. "Yes, I traveled globally... Lived in Bermuda 2 1/2 years and Singapore 2 years. Visited most western European Countries as well as most SE Asian Countries and North

Asia visiting customers and employees of our company." Referring to my own career, Stan wrote, "I too never had the slightest idea what was beyond our little world in those days. I, you, and many others learned from those humble beginnings and opened our lives to possibilities beyond our wildest dreams." After his mother passed in 2011, Stan and his wife Gretchen lived Patton, PA, near Iselin, restoring her family's old farmhouse while traveling to Iselin frequently to join in the care of his father until Alex's passing in 2013. He's happy to be living a quieter but still busy life in retirement, often helping friends with home improvements, continuing that wonderful Semuskie tradition.

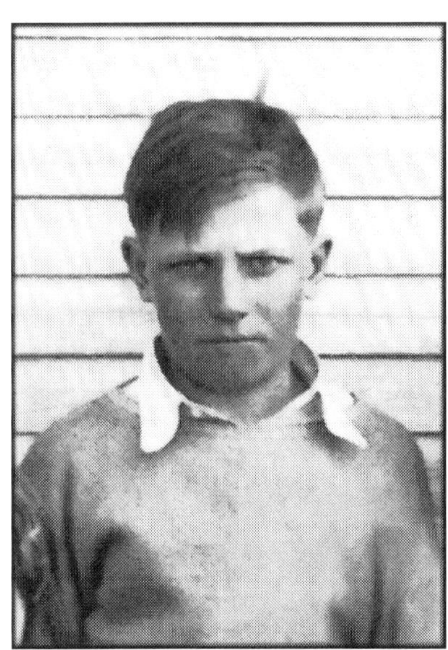

Top Left: Alex Semuskie, Grade 6, 1934
Top Right: Nellie Semuskie Knopick near the Hotel, c1946
Bottom: Alex and Edith Semuskie's formal wedding photograph

The Alex and Edith (Clements) Semuskie's Wedding Party, 1948. Jennie Clements and Dorothy Prelcz, Bridesmaids. Mike Malec and John Persarsky, Groomsmen (both from Iselin). Carolyn Morganti and Nancy Mesojedic, Young Girl Attendants.

The Semuskie boys—l to r (front) Stan, Greg, Tim, Alex with their friends (back) Larry Ditch and Emmit Bevins. "Greg broke his jaw sledding down an icy Store Hill—jaw wired shut for over a month."

Iselin from Matlack's Hill. Stan wrote, "Mike Condor and I used to go up on Matlacks Hill with a bottle of wine, some cheese, and a blanket and just sit and reminisce on warm fall days." They had not seen the 1941 movie "How Green Was My Valley"—this was an expression of "love of place" straight from their hearts.

Sunset over Iselin, photo by Stan Semuskie

18. Quote from Emery Francesco, Iselin coal miner, published in *Coal People.*

19. Obituary for James P. Lambert (1909-1981), *Indiana Evening Gazette* April 27, 1981.

Sara Lambert Bloom adds: Mr Lambert was a smart, hardworking man, devoted to family and community, attributes embedded in his DNA and nurtured in his upbringing. His great-grandfather, Michael Lambert (1820-1873) never made it to America from his home in County Waterford in Ireland but he made sure his family did. Michael would have been in his mid-twenties when Ireland suffered the potato famine that hit its peak in 1845. Over a million died in Ireland either from starvation or hunger-related disease and Ireland lost a quarter of its population with a further million emigrating to other countries. Learning this makes me feel lucky to be an American, a descendent of one of the ones who avoided starvation and made it to America. It's my family's version of the story of every Iselin family—escape to America to seek a better life. Even beyond the blight that hit the potato crop was the brutal requirement that Irish farmers export the other, unaffected crops they grew to their British landlords in England (the Irish being forbidden to own land in their own country) while watching their families suffer and die from starvation. (There's that theme of "we were owned" from the Iselin story.) There are reports of the starving Irish eating grass, and of being shot when attempting to gather mussels (that were not a marketable commodity) from the rocks. Michael Patrick Lambert II (b. 1946 in Indiana, PA) wrote in *And We'll All Go Together—An Irish Family Emigrates to America* (published 2022), "By word and by example, the American-born Lamberts and affiliated family branches were taught to conduct themselves with honor, to fear their God, and to respect authority, save perhaps for the detestable British landlords…Ethos was translated into action by this all-important second generation of American Lamberts."

James P. Lambert's own father, Michael Patrick Lambert I (1875-1934), was born in Charlestown, MA and found work that he loved as a locomotive engineer on the Baltimore, Rochester, and Pittsburgh Railroad while many of his relatives in his parents' generation worked as colliers (coal miners), mostly in Pennsylvania.

James P. Lambert's grandparents, who immigrated from Ireland in 1872, could neither read nor write but his parents were literate, although not formally educated. The style of writing in the letters that his father wrote to him in the early 1930s fairly "sings" in that lovely, lyric way of an Irish bard; to me it is reminiscent of the writing style of Sean O'Casey. Mr. Lambert's mother had received only an 8th grade education, but the importance of education was instilled in him and his seven siblings by their parents. St. Catherine High School in his hometown of DuBois, PA was the first parochial school in Pennsylvania to be accredited by the State Department of Education in 1915. Mr. Lambert was a graduate of St Catherine's in 1927, following a business track curriculum. In addition to being employed as Town Manager of Iselin by the R&P Coal Company and subsequently by Kovalchick Real Estate for most of his 40 years living in Iselin, he was an elected Justice of the Peace for Young Twp for over 25 years and, being self-taught in matters of the law, won an election in 1970 to become District Magistrate for Indiana County. He served just 4 of his 6-year term, having to retire in 1974 due to ill health. He served several terms as President of the Elders Ridge School District. Mr Lambert was a member of Holy Cross Catholic Church, a life member of the BPOE (Elks) Lodge of Apollo and was affiliated with the Lions Club of Young Township. He was a skilled carpenter, an avid hunter and trout fisherman, and an enthusiastic fan of the Pittsburgh Steelers, attending many of their home games and several Super Bowls with his wife.

And in addition to the ways in which he served the Church and School Board outside of his official duties as Town Manager and Justice of the Peace/District Magistrate, Mr Lambert always, always was thinking of the welfare of his family and neighbors and finding ways to help individuals. As they were born, he purchased a Prudential life insurance policy, for which he paid 10 cents per week for each of the five babies that he and Sara gave birth to, and presented it to them when each turned 21. He filled out their tax returns for Iselin residents who needed help. He helped his father-in-law, a self-employed blacksmith in DuBois, to buy into Social Security when that became available, which helped our Granna Hayes immeasurably when she became eligible for benefits when Granddad Hayes died. And so it was a logical leap for Mr Lambert, working as an unpaid and unrelenting advocate for social justice, to tackle Iselin's major life-threatening hazards including toxic air quality, lack of a reliable source of potable water, and lack of a sewage system.

Indiana County Municipal Services Authority's Executive Director Mike Duffalo wrote, "I cherish fond memories of your father and his work with ICMSA. He was a man of great integrity and was both a pioneer and visionary for his time."

A serious but happy person, his favorite thing was to pile his family into the car and drive to Camp Shamrock, the fishing camp that he and extended family members built on the First Fork of Sinnemahoning Creek (the area known as “God’s Country,” north of DuBois), singing to his wife in his beautiful Irish tenor voice a 1919 song made famous in the 1944 movie “When Irish Eyes Are Smiling,”:

“With someone like you, a gal good and true, I’d like to leave it all behind and go and find, a place that’s known, to God alone, just a spot to call our own. We’ll find perfect peace, where joys never cease, somewhere beneath a kindly sky. We’ll build a sweet little nest, somewhere in the west, and let the rest of the world go by.” And they did (but it was northeast of Iselin, not “somewhere in the west”).

https://www.youtube.com/watch?v=YKdDJhC8QQg

One example of his special sense of humor: “Dad had us kids watching out for a lost Indian boy when we drove past signs on those mountainous roads that warned: ‘Watch for Falling Rock.’”

An example of our special family humor: On one of those family drives during a particularly tight financial time for the family, as we approached an ice cream stand we began chanting “You scream, I scream, we all scream for ice cream.” Dad answered firmly, “You think an ice cream cone is only ten cents, but there are seven of us and that’s 70 cents and that’s almost a dollar. I don’t want to hear the word ice cream again.” Silence, giggling, whispering. Followed by our taking up a chant for “wolf-wolf,” the code word we cleverly invented for ice cream. We saw our parents exchange a look and a small smile, but their silence signaled to us that the answer was still "no."

But don't get the impression that Dad was a Scrooge! He was wisely saving money to provide exciting experiences (while teaching us to make ice cream at home for far less than an ice cream stand would charge for seven cones). The Greater Pittsburgh Airport opened on May 31, 1952, and we all piled into the family car for the 130-mile round trip from Iselin to sit in the fabulous lounge and watch in wonder as the planes took off and landed. What is today's equivalent of that thrill we shared as a family seventy one years ago? A trip to NASA's Kennedy Space Center to watch a rocket lift off? If ever a plane flew over Iselin, which was rare, my playmates and I would race, wildly waving our arms, looking up and shouting at it, "Gimme a ride!" while trying to make sense of what we were seeing.

The touching poem *Jump In Jackson* was written by singer/songwriter Ed McGee (1969-) when he was in 5th grade in Hanover, NH. Ed is a grandson of James P. Lambert and loved that his granddad called him "Jackson," the endearing nickname he called each of his grandchildren. The poem begins "Jump in Jackson, you'll ride shotgun today," and goes on to describe the joy they had riding together through the Appalachian countryside when, as a boy, Ed was invited to accompany his Granddad on his errands. Each stanza ends with, "But why can I hear him breathe?" a poetic expression of grief from a boy that serves to express the grief of all those who have lost a loved one to Black Lung disease.

And We'll All Go Together --An Irish Family Emigrates to America researched and written by Marie Lambert McGee and Michael Patrick Lambert II

20. Obituary for Sara L. Lambert (1909-2016), https://www.legacy.com/us/obituaries/triblive-valley-news-dispatch/name/sara-lambert-obituary?id=7192946

Sara Lambert Bloom adds: In 2014 Mrs Lambert asked that this invitation be published in the *Indiana Gazette*:

Family, friends, and acquaintances...the family of

Sara L. Lambert

invites you to the Lambert home in Iselin for an

105th Birthday Open House

Wednesday, Dec. 10

1:00 pm on throughout the day

All are welcome!

Please call xxx-xxx-xxxx for directions

And they came from throughout Indiana County and beyond and they stayed throughout the day!!

Michael Hood, then Dean of Fine Arts at IUP, came to the Big House in Iselin to present Mrs Lambert with a Medal welcoming her into IUP's Pioneer Society.

Photographs taken at the Celebration by Stan Semuskie can be seen on his website:

https://stan-semuskie.smugmug.com/Family/Mrs-Lamberts-105-Birthday-Party/i-ZWwwBSt

In 2015 Mrs Lambert's daughter Marie held an **Open House** at her home in Sharon, Vermont to celebrate **Sara L. Lambert's 106th Birthday** on December 10th. And once again they came from near and far and they stayed throughout the day!!

Mrs Lambert's favorite poem, *The Passing of Arthur* from the *Idylls of the King* written by Sir Alfred Lord Tennyson (1809-1892), was on her nightstand when she died at the age of 106. She could recite it some 90+ years after memorizing it in her youth. In February 2016 it was read at her funeral by her granddaughter, Julia Hale.

"The old order changeth, yielding place to new,
And God fulfils himself in many ways,
Lest one good custom should corrupt the world.
Comfort thyself: what comfort is in me?
I have lived my life, and that which I have done
May He within himself make pure! but thou,
If thou shouldst never see my face again,
Pray for my soul. More things are wrought by prayer
Than this world dreams of."

In addition to music and poetry, in her retirement years Mrs Lambert developed her talent for stitching, creating over 100 canvases in needlepoint and petit point, both landscapes and portraitures, and then learning to create portraits in sepia tones that she stitched from photographs of members of her family and friends (the photo not having been "stamped" on her blank canvas, just charted on a grid that she referenced as she stitched). She reached a high level of artistic achievement while being self-taught in this somewhat obscure but stunningly beautiful art form. More than 100 were temporarily collected from their owners for the occasion to be displayed at the concert performed in Gorell Hall at IUP to celebrate her 80th birthday and some again were displayed at her wake.

Add trout fishing and playing cribbage (passions that she taught to her children and grandchildren and great-grandchildren), following the Pittsburgh Steelers, including several trips to the Super Bowl with her husband, and mothering and grandmothering, and always teaching to get closer to a complete portrait of Sara LaRue (Hayes) Lambert; add kind and caring and gentle to a description of her personal attributes.

Sara and Elizabeth, her first cousin once removed, were members of two of the large number of Hayes families living in and around DuBois and Force, PA. Born just 2 years apart, they were frequent companions in their youth. "First cousin once removed" is the term used for Elizabeth being a first cousin of Sara's father, Byron Leolin Hayes (Barney) who was a self-employed blacksmith working out of his shop at the lower edge of the back yard of their house on Wilson Avenue in Sandy Township, just outside of DuBois. Barney's work was primarily shoeing horses and repairing tools in the early 1900s and when the automobile became the mode of transportation, the forge of Barney Hayes Blacksmith became the source of some of the loveliest iron fences and railings in all of Clearfield County. Sara's mother, Estelle (Stella) Platt Hayes, saved money in a teapot, money she called her "egg money," to send three of her five children to college. Sara was 8 years old when her mother bought the baby grand piano that held a place of honor in their living room for 50 years. Called Granna by her grandchildren, Stella could ride a horse as well as Tom Mix (1880-1940), who grew up in DuBois and became the star of many Western films, while Sara preferred staying home to immerse herself in music and poetry and literature. But Sara loved that her only Hayes niece, Annette Hayes Williams, was an excellent equestrian who owned and rode horses well into her 80s. Annette remembers fondly her frequent visits with her Iselin cousins at her Aunt Sara's invitation, loving the time she spent in the Big House and surrounding fields. She reminded me recently that everyone worried when I got a tummy ache when I was little from eating too many cherries that I had picked from our trees—so excited that they were finally ripe! Now that's a 74-year-old memory that shouts love and caring and family! I can't believe that Annette remembers it; I don't! (But were they really ripe yet?)

When the two-part tribute to Dr Elizabeth Hayes (far more than an obituary) was published in the DuBois newspaper when Dr Betty died in 1984, my mother sent copies to me, inscribing on the back, "This is the stuff you are made of." Although I knew that my mother and father were pleased with my success as a professional oboist and teacher, my having just been appointed Professor of Oboe at the Cincinnati Conservatory of Music and being immersed in giving performances across America and abroad, I always knew that they expected me to follow in the family's quest for social justice any time I saw the need and the opportunity to step up and do something. It's wonderful that retirement from my music career is allowing me to work pro bono on some very important social justice missions.

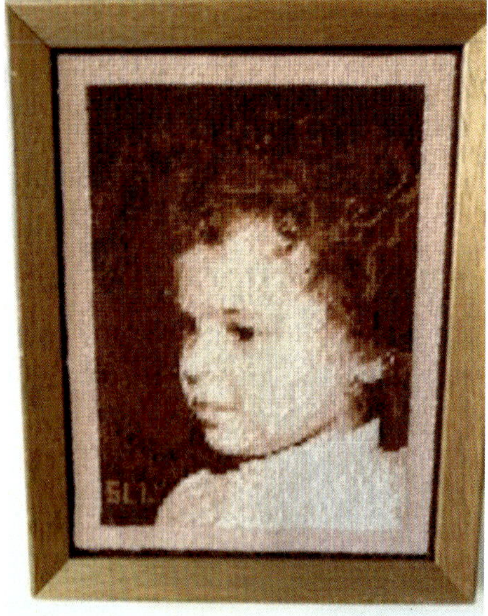

Needlepoint portrait in sepia tones

A second needlepoint portrait

My mother loved working on this canvas that I brought back from Austria when I visited the birthplace of Wolfgang Amadeus Mozart while on tour in Europe. We never got it matted and framed but I love it as is.

Needlepoint frame she created for her 1929 IUP graduation photo and the rose she created, giving one to each of her 5 children in the 1980s to celebrate the Semuskies' beautiful, transformative renovation of the "Rose Room" in the Big House.

My husband built this headboard and my mother created Sweet Dreams in needlepoint when our little daughter transitioned from her crib to her big girl bed in 1981. It is now used as a bookcase. The tall bell is the School Bell that my mother used in her first teaching position in 1929 to call the pupils in.

Top Right: My mother created this needlepoint when she returned to Iselin after hearing me play the famous English horn solo composed by Jean Sibelius titled the Swan of Tuonela with New Haven Symphony Orchestra. My husband made the frame, painting the border white.

Bottom Right: A commendation from Pennsylvania's Governor Robert P. Casey, Sr, on her 80th Birthday

Commonwealth of Pennsylvania

Governor's Office

105th Birthday Celebration in Iselin, with her daughters Marie and Jane and her son John

The Pioneer Society Medal from IUP, presented to her by Michael Hood, Dean of Fine Arts

Invitation to her 106th Birthday Open House in Vermont

Mrs Lambert trout fishing with her 5 children,
l to r Jim, Sally, Jane, Marie, John

21. Sara Lambert Bloom (1944-) writes: I was raised in Iselin along with my four older siblings Jane, Marie, James M., and John, children of James P. Lambert, Iselin's Town Manager, and his wife Sara. I consider it a life-forming event that I became the paid organist for daily Mass and one of the two Sunday Masses at Iselin's Holy Cross Church. Beginning when I was 11 years old, I played and sang (alone) the Gregorian Mass in Latin until I left to attend the Oberlin Conservatory where I earned the Bachelor of Music degree, graduating Pi Kappa Lambda, becoming a professional oboist after attending the Yale School of Music for my graduate studies, where I earned a Master of Music degree in 1968. As a church organist, I was asked by the priest to add the *Dies Irae* to the many funeral Masses I sang and played for those, mostly coal miners, who died during my childhood years in Iselin. It is one of the most famous sequences of Gregorian chant, *Dies Irae* – "Day of Wrath" – describing the Last Judgment of souls before God where the saved will go to heaven and the unsaved will be cast into eternal flames of suffering, which I now admit frightened me at the time.

For our one-half-hour daily Mass I sang and played only four movements of the Gregorian Mass (the Introitus-Requiem Aeternam, the Kyrie, the Sanctus, and the Agnus Dei), adding the Dies Irae only for the longer funeral service:

https://youtu.be/vDcrY7cuHYw.

I shall never forget the funeral of a darling 3-year-old girl. Just moments before the funeral Mass began, her mother came to me, her eyes filled with tears, telling me that her little daughter was afraid of the organ, so I sang the entire funeral Mass, the *Missa pro Defunctis* in Latin acapella, my eyes filled with tears.

I feel honored to have been included at such an early age as a junior organist, in the succession of three senior organists at Holy Cross Church over its 86-year history, beginning with (the late) Rose Patterson Dowdell, through the wonderful 50 years of service offered with joy and grace by (the late) Erma Francisco as senior organist and choir master from 1931 until her retirement in 1981, followed by devoted organist Ruth Rogel who held that position until the Church was closed by the Greensburg Diocese in 1989.

During my youth in Iselin, music was not my only interest. I enjoyed academics, graduating Valedictorian of my Elders Ridge High School class of 1962, was Co-Captain of our wonderful ERHS girls' basketball team, and in general enjoyed the "free range" activities with my playmates that life in Iselin offered us, like riding bikes and learning to ski and anything we could dream up that did not require spending money or having transportation out of Iselin. And I loved all the Lambert family activities like learning to play cards and to catch a trout and to bake and to sew on my Gramma Bess's treadle, all of which I continue today with the exception of skiing and with the substitution of Pickle Ball for basketball!

I researched, conducted interviews, searched for vintage photographs, and wrote this book to honor my heritage.

Oboist, teacher, mentor, author, editor, commissioning and recording artist; advocate for social justice, I can be found in the World Biographical Encyclopedia and am listed as a noteworthy oboist and teacher by the Marquis *Who's Who*, which was founded in 1898.

My CV includes Professor of Oboe, retired, Cincinnati Conservatory of Music; Artist-faculty, retired, Aspen Music Festival and Sarasota Music Festival; Artistic Director, retired, Music from Cranberry Isles; Recipient, NEA Consortium Commissioning grant; Trustee, Chamber Music America; Charter Member, US Holocaust Memorial Museum

I am producer and musical collaborator on the 7-CD archive of live performances titled *The Art of Robert Bloom*, released on Boston Records label in 1999-2000 and now available on our website: RobertandSaraLambertBloom.com

Quoting a review of *The Art of Robert Bloom* written by Bernard Jacobson, Program Annotator and Musicologist for the Philadelphia Orchestra and Artistic Director, Residentie Orkest, The Hague, writing for *Fanfare Magazine:* Calling Bloom's playing cynosure, or brilliant enough to navigate by, Jacobson writes: “Legends from the Golden Past turn out sadly often, on close present-day examination, to be legendary and no more, and invested with the gilt of spurious greatness only by the glow of nostalgia. Let me not needlessly raise hackles by offering a few example that, in my estimation, belong in this category--regular readers can probably supply some names without my repeating them. Suffice it to say that Robert Bloom, oboist, composer, conductor, teacher, and editor, emerges from these volumes of an ambitious retrospective set of recordings as a blessed exception...These discs show us a player of phenomenal gifts, not merely technical, though in that sphere he can have had few rivals, but in the fields of musicianship, of expressivity, and also--a salutary revelation in these days when we think we are the first generation to have discovered the truth about Baroque style--of taste in the interpretation and embellishment of 18th-century texts.”

My piano lessons began very early. With her husband's blessing, my mother provided lessons for me and my older siblings with beloved (the late) Sister Elizabeth, a member of the St Joseph's order. The trip was sometimes arduous, my mother driving through snow and storm on winding hilly roads. The five of us lined up for our piano lessons at the convent connected with the school that was adjacent to and affiliated with St Bernard of Clairvaux Parish in Indiana and lined up at home to practice our assignments daily on the classic upright piano we had inherited from our great-grandmother Sarah Jane Platt. I still have my prized possessions, my first piano primers, *Cubby* and *More About Cubby.* My first oboe was lent to me by the visiting music teacher, (the late) Samuel P. Catalino, when I was a sixth grader attending the Iselin Elementary School in 1956. Over the next six years (the late) Mr Samuel Catalino "carted" me around the state as I won oboe auditions and was selected for County, District, and All-State Band and Orchestra and (as a singer) Choral Festivals, my proud parents never failing to attend these exciting events. I remember that my father would call out to me as I left home for one of these instrumental festivals, "Blow hard and follow the notes," his self-deprecating way of encouraging me without having the slightest idea of how I was achieving success as a fledgling oboist. And then at the end of a weekend away spent rehearsing and making new friends, I could always count on looking out at the audience members who came to the performance and see Dad waving his program to let me know that he and my mother were there. Mr Catalino suggested that his sister, Rosalie, give me private lessons in piano and music theory at our home during those formative summers, which helped my musical development enormously. Rosalie graduated from Seton Hill College and went on to enjoy a wonderful career in music before passing away much too early. At my high school graduation, Mr Catalino presented me with the first John Philips Sousa Award given to an outstanding musician at Elders Ridge High School, where he was the devoted and much beloved Band Director. Prior to attending Oberlin and Yale, I continued my musical studies during my high school years, taking private oboe lessons with (the late) Professor Daniel DiCicco and piano and voice lessons with (the late) Professor, Dr Russel C. Nelson, both highly respected members of the music faculty at IUP.

Teachers are a gift to humanity.

Like my wonderful parents, my teachers did not urge me to reach for the stars. They wisely fed me appropriate opportunities and wanted for me only to humbly take one opportunity at a time and make it beautiful and meaningful to those who listened to my music-making. And they taught me to love and be grateful for the privilege of being able to do that, if I worked hard enough. The noble spirit of Iselin shaped every phrase I played.

After I finished high school, my parents continued to travel faithfully to hear my student concerts at Oberlin, Yale, Dartmouth, Monteux Festival, and SUNY at Binghamton, and professional appearances in New Haven, New York, Sarasota, Aspen, Cincinnati, and Cranberry Island (but alas, not my European appearances). My father once said he was going to have to hang a cowbell around my neck so he could keep track of where I was performing.

I stepped in for my sister Jane when she became ill in early 2015 and expanded my pattern of making visits to Iselin to spend time with my mother to join Marie to tag-team as our mother's full-time caregivers at Marie's home. I commuted to Sharon VT from my home in Maine to spend each weekend there, participating in what I consider one of life's most precious phases of being. As it happened, I was visiting Jane in Salt Lake City when Mom died in Vermont, so the four of us were together virtually for those moments of her passage. Sadly, Jane died at her home in Salt Lake City surrounded by her loved ones, including Marie, just 5 weeks after Mom died in Vermont at the age of 106 in 2016.

My mother-in-law and father-in-law, Ida Fisher Bloom (1876-1930) and Julius Bloom (1872-1942), escaped the pogroms happening in and around their homes in Kiev as teenagers, emigrating to America in the late 1880s (just before Ellis Island became our port of entry). Settling in Pittsburgh where they married and raised 7 children including my late husband Robert (1908-1994), Cantor Julius Bloom held a position with several synagogues in Pittsburgh.

An interesting connection: Frank Gorell, Indiana (PA) industrialist/businessman and benefactor to IUP and the Pittsburgh Symphony Orchestra, among many other institutions, was a boy soloist in Cantor Bloom's synagogue choir, often in his youth singing sacred songs at the High Holidays that Cantor Bloom composed specifically for his young star. Before his passing in 2006, Frank let me know that Cantor Bloom wrote those solos for him, but not for his own son, Robert! Frank was indeed a very talented singer and an accomplished French horn player who, after graduating from the Curtis Institute of Music as a student of the French horn, briefly explored the opportunity of becoming "The Tommy Dorsey of the French horn" by combining his instrumental and singing talents as a soloist with the popular orchestra of that era conducted by Paul

Whiteman. After holding positions in the Navy Band in Washington DC, in the Pittsburgh and Baltimore Symphony Orchestras, and on staff in NYC for both the CBS and NBC radio broadcasts, Frank left his professional career in music to become an industrialist, eventually locating his business in Indiana, PA.

Back in 1923, Robert and Frank were members of the choir that Cantor Bloom led in singing the traditional *S'eu shearin* to consecrate the third and last synagogue he served, B'nai Israel on Negley Avenue. In a parallel to the story of Iselin, the congregation of this synagogue merged with Adath Sha'om in Fox Chapel in 2000 and like Iselin's Holy Cross Church, their historic building, B'nai Israel, that was once a consecrated synagogue, was desanctified and is being converted into residential apartments.

Of the 20+ new works that I commissioned, the one I most cherish is a serious work that I asked a celebrated California-based composer, Joel Feigin to write for me in anticipation of the occasion of the 50th anniversary of the liberation of Auschwitz in 1995. He titled the trio for oboe, viola, and piano *Echoes from the Holocaust.* Although I took early retirement before being able to record it for Centaur label where many of my recordings can be found, an audio recording captured my live performance at an international conference at Indiana University in Bloomington:

https://www.youtube.com/watch?v=78uSnxS1tKo

One reviewer wrote: "Sara Lambert Bloom's masterful performance of *Echoes from the Holocaust* was not about fingering, intonation, or dynamics. The composer and musician succeeded in not merely making good music or painting a picture. Shockingly they were able to creep inside our souls. Sara Bloom's dynamic performance mystifies me. It is beyond my experience of life for a piece of music to be able to transcend being good music to being capable of releasing and creating historical tension.”

I remember fondly one of my Iselin playmates, the youngest of five beautiful sisters. We didn’t spend much time at her house. Her father mostly sat on the porch glider in all but wintertime, a kind man with a frightening cough and a concave chest from a mine accident. Lying on our backs in a beautiful meadow one summer day, looking up at the clouds, one of us asked, “Do you think we’ll ever see the ocean?’ and we laughed, dismissing such a notion, and got back to finding shapes in the clouds. I remember fondly telling that story to my husband, Robert. At the time we were sitting in the marbled cocktail lounge at the top of the Athens Hilton, looking down on the Acropolis. Sometimes I can’t believe that all of this happened to me, loving every bit of it, but I believe that this book explains how and why it did happen and how much I owe to Iselin.

And yes, they all wept as I played and sang the *Missa pro Defunctis*, including the *Dies Irae*, as our priest officiated at the funeral of my little friend’s father in Iselin’s Holy Cross Church.

Sally's first communion, 1950

Sally Lambert and Erma Francisco, Jr and Sr Organists, 1958

Sara Lambert Bloom, Oboist, photo by Sheldon Secunda, 1991

Robert Bloom, far left, just after conducting Mozart K. 297b at the Aspen Music Festival with orchestra and 4 soloists, including his oboist wife, Sara, along with her colleagues, the late Leonard Sharrow, bassoon, Robin Graham, French horn, and Richard Waller, clarinet, in 1975. After Robert retired from his career performing as the solo English hornist of the Philadelphia Orchestra under the baton of Maestro Leopold Stokowski, the solo oboist of the NBC Symphony Orchestra under Maestro Arturo Toscanini, making over 200 commercial recordings as the principal oboist of the RCA Victor and Columbia Symphony Orchestras under the batons of Maestros Stokowski, Reiner, Shaw, Bernstein, Steinberg, Stravinsky, Iturbi, Fiedler, and other leading conductors of the day, and recording and touring nationally and internationally as the solo oboist of the Bach Aria Group under the direction of William H. Scheide, Robert enjoyed a "second act" career as a conductor before his passing in 1994. Among several other teaching appointments, Robert was a member of the Major Faculty at the Juilliard School of Music and Professor of Oboe at the Yale School of Music where he taught Sara during her studies to earn a Master of Music degree in Oboe Performance. He was a native of Pittsburgh. The Blooms collaborated frequently as performers and teachers.

Backstage with Mom and Dad after my solo performance at the Aspen (CO) Music Festival, 1975

Notes

Prologue

1."Coal Mining," https://en.wikipedia.org/wiki/Coal_mining

Chapter 2 The Need for Coal

1. James B. Jones, Jr., "Coal Mining in the Cumberland Plateau, 1880-1930," *National Park Services: Appalachian Cultural Resources Workshop Papers* (1880-1930), 2008.

Chapter 3 My Mission As an Author and My Growth As a Person

1. Adrian Georg Iselin, Jr. (1846-1935), https://en.wikipedia.org/wiki/Adrian_Iselin_Jr

2. "It's a Wonderful Life," is a 1946 film produce and directed by Frank Capra. It was nominated for five Academy Awards, including Best Picture, and has been recognized by the American Film Institute as one of the 100 best American films ever made; in 1990, "It's a Wonderful Life" was designated as "culturally, historically or aesthetically significant" and added to the National Film Registry of the Library of Congress. Its significance to the story of Iselin

having been owned is a story line in the movie that is perhaps secondary to the main character's thoughts of suicide and the earning of angels' wings. But the avaricious Henry Potter's attempts to control even more of Bedford Falls by shutting down the beneficent Bailey Brothers Building and Loan drives the story of this classic movie. Is it a coincidence that the film's star, James Stewart (1908-1997) as George Bailey, was born and raised in Indiana, PA?

3. Elizabeth Cocke writes in "The Company Coal Towns of Central Pennsylvania: The Early Years," *Coal People, Contemporary Images of Northern Appalachia* (Indiana, PA: Printed by Nupp Printing Co., 1995), "Leisure was another arena in which companies covered their control with a layer of benevolence. Companies like R&P…built baseball fields and provided uniforms, equipment, and travel expenses for company baseball leagues. Coal companies also built playgrounds, provided uniforms and instruments for company-sponsored bands, and held company picnics on patriotic holidays. During the World War I era, many coal companies upgraded the leisure facilities in their communities, adding nickelodeons and 'amusement halls.' Correspondence between the supervisors and owners of the R&P coal company makes it clear that these improvements were motivated less by a paternalistic interest in the quality of life in their communities than by the desire to 'attract and hold a better quality of labor' in a period of labor scarcity."

She continues, "Charges of voting irregularities against coal companies were not uncommon, as it was received wisdom that, in a company town, a miner's vote was virtually a condition of employment."

Chapter 4 The Beginnings of Iselin

1. Adrian Georg Iselin (1818-1905), https://en.wikipedia.org/wiki/Adrian_Iselin

2. Julia Ann Rosborough (1844-1926),

https://wc.rootsweb.com/trees/153028/I02581/james-rosborough/individual

3. Elders Ridge (PA) Academy, https://apollopahistory.com/elders-ridge-academy/

4. Adrian Georg Iselin, Jr. (1846-1935), Wiki.

5. Iselin, Pennsylvania, an unincorporated community in Young Township, Indiana County, Pennsylvania, United States, https://en.wikipedia.org/wiki/Iselin,_Pennsylvania

6. "Horse-drawn railways," https://en.wikipedia.org/wiki/List_of_horse-drawn_railway

7. Susan Ferrandiz, *McIntyre, Pennsylvania, The Everyday Life Of A Coal Mining Company Town: 1910-1947 (photos, documents, memories of town residents)*, 2001, http://204.235.148.201/history_of_mcintyre.htm

8. Elizabeth Cocke, "The Company Coal Towns of Central Pennsylvania: The Early Years."

9. Chris DellaMea, *Iselin, PA*, coalcampusa.com

10. James M. Lambert, Essay, "Will and Ned Gribbon."

11. Marie Lambert McGee, "They called him Mr. Jim," Essay, Chapter 12, *Iselin*, 2022.

12. Eileen Mountjoy, *The Company Town of Iselin*, Special Collections and Community Archives at Indiana University of Pennsylvania, iup.edu/library/departments/archives/coal/mines-and-company-towns/the-company-town-of-iselin.html

13. Susan Hutchison Tassin, *Pennsylvania Ghost Towns: Uncovering The Hidden Past* (Mechanicsburg, PA: Stackpole Books, 2007).

14. Anthony F. C. Wallace, *Patch Towns*, amphilsoc.org

Chapter 5 The Churches

1. Jane Lambert Abe, "History of the Parish," written for *Golden Jubilee of Holy Cross Catholic Church, Iselin, Pennsylvania*

1908-1958, a booklet printed by the Church, 1958 and published as "Church History" in an article titled "Golden Jubilee Celebration Set Sunday at Iselin Holy Cross Catholic Church." (Indiana, PA: *Indiana Evening Gazette*, June 1958).

2. Andrea Jean Ploskunak Hallman, personal memory.

3. Jane (Mrs Daniel T.) Heyer, Quote from a letter printed in the booklet, *Golden Jubilee of Holy Cross Catholic Church*, *Iselin, Pennsylvania 1908-1958.*

4. Quotes from *Diamond Jubilee of Holy Cross Church, Iselin, PA (1908-1983)*, a booklet printed by the Church, 1983.

5. Tim Semuskie, personal memory.

6. Diana Heard Suman, personal memory.

7. Cocke, "The Company Coal Towns of Central Pennsylvania: The Early Years."

8. Mary Menotti Abbati personal memory.

9. Ruth Durand Shields, personal memory.

10. Church of the Good Shepherd Parish, Kent, PA, goodshepherd-kent.org/

Chapter 6 Secular Societies

1. Alex Semuskie, personal memory.

Chapter 7 Social Stratification

1. Mountjoy, *The Company Town of Iselin.*

2. Abbati, personal memory.

Chapter 8 The Housing

1. Cocke, “The Company Coal Towns of Central Pennsylvania: The Early Years.”

2. https://en.wikipedia.org/wiki/How_Green_Was_My_Valley_(film)

3. Hallman, personal memory.

4. Abbati, personal memory.

5. Mountjoy, *The Company Town of Iselin.*

6. “Frequency - DJT Electrical Training” https://studylib.net/doc/18177617/frequency---djt-electrical-training

7. Shields, personal memory.

Chapter 9 A Lasting Memorial Sets the Cemetery’s Traditions

1. Mountjoy, *The Company Town of Iselin.*

2. Tassin, *Pennsylvania Ghost Towns.*

3. A. Semuskie, personal memory.

4. Catherine Steffenino Miller, personal memory.

5. Minerva (Herky) Durand Balcome, personal memory.

6. Abbati, personal memory.

7. Debra Semuskie, personal memory.

Chapter 10 Living With Conditions in Iselin

1. Abbati, personal memory.

2. Sara Lambert Bloom, personal memory.

3. Hallman, personal memory.

4. Mountjoy, *The Company Town of Iselin*

Chapter 11 Civic Developments, including the Indiana County Hospital and the Iselin Elementary School

1. Mountjoy, *The Company Town of Iselin.*

2. Bloom, personal memory.

3. Suman, personal memory.

4. Abbati, personal memory.

5. Stan Semuskie, personal memory.

6. Dorothy Knopick Parchinsky, personal memory.

7. A. Semuskie, personal memory.

8. Hallman, personal memory.

9. Merle Travis, *Sixteen Tons*, https://www.youtube.com/watch?v=5pfVvqLM_e4

Chapter 12 James P. Lambert (1909-1981)

1. Bloom personal memory.

2. Shields, personal memory.

3. McGee, "They called him Mr Jim."

4. Ferrandiz, *McIntyre, Pennsylvania.*

5. Matt Loy, supplemented by Matthew R. Hengeveld, *The Legend of the Molly Maguires*, The Pennsylvaia State University, 2021

6. Abbati, personal memory.

7. Eileen Mountjoy Cooper, "Whiskey Run: Where Coal Dust Mixed With Murder," Oral History Feature Category of *Pennsylvania Heritage*, Spring 1980.

8. Suman, personal memory.

Chapter 13 The Kovalchick Era Begins

1. Obituary for Nick Kolavchick (1906-1977),

https://oaklandcemetery.us/profile/nick-kovalchick/

2. Bloom, personal memory.

3. Abbati, personal memory.

4. A. Semuskie, personal memory.

Chapter 14 Pursuit of Public Health Improvements for Iselin

1. Abbati, personal memory.

2. T. Semuskie, personal memory.

3. S. Semuskie, personal memory.

4. Marcia Biederman, *A Mighty Force-Dr Elizabeth Hayes and her War for Public Health.* (Landham, MD: Prometheus Books, 2021).

Chapter 15 Operation Scarlift: The first of three phases of improvements for Iselin achieved by James P. Lambert and colleagues working as unpaid citizen advocates

1. "Operation Scarlift and Mine Reclamation in Pennsylvania," Pennsylvania Department of Environmental Protection, https://www.dep.pa.gov/Business/Land/Mining/AbandonedMineReclamation/OperationScarlift/Pages/default.aspx

2. Stan Semuskie, "There was another special thing about Iselin," Essay, Chapter 15, *Iselin*, 2022.

3. Hallman, personal memory.

4. "Sulfur Dioxide," Queensland Government, last reviewed June 2022, https://www.qld.gov.au/environment/management/monitor-

ing/air/air-pollution/pollutants/sulfur-dioxide

5. “Sulfur Dioxide and Coal,” Global Energy Monitor, last edited April 2021, https://www.gem.wiki/Sulfur_dioxide_and_coal

6. “How Coal Works,” *Union of Concerned Scientists*, last updated December 2017, https://www.ucsusa.org/resources/how-coal-works

7. Matthew Brown, “Judge revives Obama-era ban on coal sales from federal lands,” *Columbian*, Billings, MT, August 2022.

8. Cassandra Clark, the study’s first author: “Proximity to fracking sites associated with risk of childhood cancer,” *Environmental Health Perspectives*, August 2022. https://ehp.niehs.nih.gov/doi/10.1289/EHP11092

Chapter 16 The Water Renovation Project: The second phase completed by Mr Lambert and his colleagues on the ICMSA, all unpaid citizen advocates

1. Indiana County Municipal Services Authority, http://icomsa.org/About-Us/ICMSA-About-Us

2. Carl Kologie, “Ribbon-Cutting Ceremony For Water Renovation Project” written by the Assistant Editor of the *Indiana Evening Gazette*. (Indiana, PA: *Indiana Evening Gazette*, January 12, 1981).

Chapter 17 A Sewage System for Iselin: Phase three realized a few short years after Mr Lambert’s passing

1. “Privies,” *Monticello*, monticello.org/research-education/thomas-jefferson-encyclopedia/privies/

2. Sue Bowman, “Pondering the Privy—A History of Outhouses.” (Lancaster, PA: *Lancaster Farming*, updated July 2022), https://www.lancasterfarming.com/

3. Photos of the groundbreaking of the Iselin Sewage Demon-

stration Project, the Dedication to the late James P. Lambert by Michael Buffalo, ED of the ICMSA, and the celebration at the Big House, Summer 1982.

4. Drawing of the Iselin Artificial Wetlands Treatment Scheme from James T. Watson, Foster D. Diodato, and Milt Lauch. "Design and Performance of the Artificial Wetlands Wastewater Treatment Plant at Iselin, Pennsylvania," *Tennessee Valley Authority, Office of Natural Resources and Economic Development*, a government publication. (Chattanooga, Tennessee: July 1986, revised December 1986).

5. Watson, Diodato, and Lauch. "Design and Performance of the Artificial Wetlands"

6. Photo, Iselin Marsh Pond Replacement Project, 1994.

Chapter 18 The Iselin Lamberts

1. "Injuries, Illnesses, and Fatalities," US Bureau of Labor Statistics, last modified May 2019,

https://www.bls.gov/iif/oshwc/osh/os/osar0012.htm#:~:text=-Coal%20mining%20is%20a%20relatively,the%20Bureau%20of%20Labor%20Statistics

2. "Coal Mining," Wiki.

3. Ferrandiz, *McIntyre, Pennsylvania.*

4. Quote from Emery Francesco, Iselin coal miner, in August 1991 for James W. Harris, "A Picture Essay," *Coal People, Contemporary Images of Northern Appalachia* (Indiana, PA: Printed by Nupp Printing Co., 1995).

5. Obituary for Sara L. Lambert (1909-2016),

https://www.legacy.com/us/obituaries/triblive-valley-news-dispatch/name/sara-lambert-obituary?id=7192946

6. Bloom, personal memory.

7. Marie Lambert McGee, personal memory.

8. Note from the author: During her final decade my mother often called me to see if I had tuned into our favorite TV news show, *Washington Week in Review* hosted by Gwen Ifill, or to see if I was watching the NY Philharmonic's broadcast, especially if it featured the celebrated soprano Renée Fleming. Ms Fleming was born in 1959 in "our" Indiana County General Hospital, built for us coal people in 1914 by Adrian Iselin Jr, when her parents, Edwin Fleming and Patricia (Seymour) Alexander were vocal music students enrolled at IUP, in fact being members of my sister Marie's class at IUP. Or Mom would call to tell me that she was watching a broadcast of the Pittsburgh Symphony Orchestra and could pick out one of my colleagues from Yale, the Orchestra's dynamic principal cellist, Anne Martindale Williams. So to celebrate my mother's 99th birthday I invited Anne to Iselin to play for a small gathering of Mom's friends and relatives, in the living room of her "Big House." Anne performed several movements from Bach's famous unaccompanied Cello Suite No. 1, and there wasn't a dry eye in the house. Anne shared with me her surprise that a town like Iselin still existed in 2008, and so close to Pittsburgh—she said that her visit to Iselin was like traveling back a century in time to visit a European village. My late husband, Robert Bloom, was also charmed by his many visits to Iselin. People who have performed everywhere from Carnegie Hall to major concert halls around the world appreciated immediately the rare goodness and genuine authenticity of our town and its residents.

Chapter 19 A Family's Devotion To Public Health

1. Woody Guthrie, *The Dying Doctor*, https://www.woodyguthrie.org/Lyrics/Dying_Doctor.htm

2. "Dr. Betty Hayes (1912-1984) and her father, Dr Leo Zeno Hayes (1878-1942)," Mt Zion Historical Society,

https://mtzionhistoricalsociety.org/history/stories/the-valleys-coal-miners-doctor/

3. Obituary for Elizabeth Hayes, MD (1912-1984),

https://www.nytimes.com/2022/04/01/obituaries/elizabeth-hayes-overlooked.html

4. Biederman. *A Mighty Force*

Chapter 20 Getting Back to Iselin's Public Health Journey

1. ICMSA, http://icomsa.org/About-Us/ICMSA-About-Us

2. Obituary for James P. Lambert (1909-1981), *Indiana Evening Gazette* April 27, 1981.

Chapter 21 The Cover Of This Book

1. Photo of Iselin, nestled in the rolling hills of Appalachia.

2. Vintage photo of the Iselin Power House, Tipple, and Pig's Ear, 1904.

3. Photos of the groundbreaking of the Iselin Sewage Demonstration Project, the Dedication to the late James P. Lambert by Michael Buffalo, ED of the ICMSA, and the celebration at the Big House, Summer 1982.

4. ICMSA, http://icomsa.org/About-Us/ICMSA-About-Us

5. Formal photo of James P. Lambert.

6. Bloom, personal memory.

Chapter 22 The "Big House"

1. Marie Lambert McGee, *WPML Seller Disclosure Statement Attachment A* written by Marie Lambert McGee (1939-), Administrator for the Estate of Sara L. Lambert, her mother.

2. James M. Lambert. Essay on the construction of the Rosborough farmhouse contributed to *WPML Seller Disclosure Statement Attachment A* written by his sister, Marie Lambert McGee; reprinted

in Chapter 22, *Iselin*, 2022

Chapter 23 Not Ready To Be Called A "Ghost Town"

1. Bloom, personal memory.

2. Larry Askins, personal memory.

3. "Pennsylvania has the most abandoned coal mines in the U.S.," *WITF Let's Discover*, https://www.witf.org/2022/02/10/pennsylvania-has-the-most-abandoned-coal-mines-in-the-u-s-how-245-million-will-help/#

4. Hallman, personal memory.

5. A. Semuskie, personal memory.

6. S. Semuskie, https://stan-semuskie.smugmug.com/Family/Bottleworks-gallery

https://stan-semuskie.smugmug.com/Photo-Restorations/Iselin-Pennsylvania

https://stan-semuskie.smugmug.com/Family/Mrs-Lamberts-105-Birthday-Party/i-ZWwwBSt

Epilogue
(Notes for 18 of the 21 entries)

1. Ferrandiz, *McIntyre, Pennsylvania.*

2. Eileen Mountjoy, "Iselin Family," part of the series Coal Culture: People, Lives, and Stories, Indiana University of Pennsyvania, 1981, https://www.iup.edu/library/departments/archives/coal/people-lives-stories/iselin-family.htm

3. "Project Zero," *The Theory of Multiple Intelligences*,

http://www.pz.harvard.edu/projects/multiple-intelligences

Abe, "History of the Parish."

4. *Golden Jubilee of Holy Cross Catholic Church*

5. Cook Forest State Park,

https://www.dcnr.pa.gov/StateParks/FindAPark/CookForestState-Park/Pages/default.aspx

http://electrical-science.blogspot.com/2009/12/history-of-power-frequency.html?m=1

6. Jospeh Abbati, https://josephabbati.art

7. https://www.secretservice.gov/

8. Bill Perry, fine arts painter. BillPerryPaintings.com

https://stan-semuskie.smugmug.com/Family/Bottleworks-gallery

10. ICMSA , http://icomsa.org/About-Us/ICMSA-About-Us

12. The William I. Heard Memorial Scholarship Award, https://www.iup.edu/cbpe/iup-difference/awards-and-scholarships/william-heard-memorial-scholarship.html

13. Healthcare Financial Management Association, https://www.hfma.org/

14. Canterbury Coal accident, https://www.themilitant.com/2000/6402/640259.html

15. ICMSA.

17. S. Semuskie, https://stan-semuskie.smugmug.com/Family/Bottleworks-gallery

https://stan-semuskie.smugmug.com/Photo-Restorations/Iselin-Pennsylvania

https://stan-semuskie.smugmug.com/Family/Mrs-Lamberts-105-Birthday-Party/i-ZWwwBSt

18. Harris, "A Picture Essay," *Coal People.*

19. Obituary for James P. Lambert (1909-1981).

ICMSA.

Justice of the Peace, https://www.pa-roots.com

District Magistrate, https://www.pacourts.us/courts/courts-of-common-pleas/individual-county-courts/indiana-county

20. Obituary for Sara L. Lambert (1909-2016).

Pioneer Society, IUP.

21. RobertandSaraLambertBloom.com

Bibliography

Focus articles:

Adrian Georg Iselin (1818-1905), https://en.wikipedia.org/wiki/Adrian_Iselin

Adrian Iselin, Jr (1846-1935), https://en.wikipedia.org/wiki/Adrian_Iselin_Jr

Coal Mining, https://en.wikipedia.org/wiki/Coal_mining

Elders Ridge (PA) Academy, https://apollopahistory.com/elders-ridge-academy/

Iselin, Pennsylvania, an unincorporated community in Young Township, Indiana County, Pennsylvania, United States, https://en.wikipedia.org/wiki/Iselin,_Pennsylvania

Julia Ann Rosborough (1844-1926), https://wc.rootsweb.com/trees/153028/I02581/james-rosborough/individual

Books, articles, essays, a Master's degree dissertation, a Postdoctoral research paper, lyrics intended for a song, and lyrics for a song that reached #1 on the Billboard charts:

Abe, Jane Lambert. "History of the Parish," published in *Golden Jubilee of Holy Cross Catholic Church, Iselin, Pennsylvania 1908-1958*, a booklet printed by the Church, 1958 and reprinted as "Church History" in an article titled "Golden Jubilee Celebration Set Sunday at Iselin Holy Cross Catholic Church." (Indiana, PA: *Indiana Evening Gazette,* June 1958).

Biederman, Marcia. *A Mighty Force-Dr Elizabeth Hayes and her War for Public Health.* (Landham, MD: Prometheus Books, 2021), https://marciabiederman.com/

Bowman, Sue. "Pondering the Privy—A History of Outhouses" (Lancaster, PA: *Lancaster Farming*, updated July 2022), https://www.lancasterfarming.com/

Brown, Matthew. "Judge revives Obama-era ban on coal sales from federal lands," *Columbian*, Billings, MT, August 2022.

Clark, Cassandra, the study's first author. "Proximity to fracking sites associated with risk of childhood cancer," *Environmental Health Perspectives*, August 2022. https://ehp.niehs.nih.gov/doi/10.1289/EHP11092

Cocke, Elizabeth. "The Company Coal Towns of Central Pennsylvania: The Early Years," *Coal People, Contemporary Images of Northern Appalachia* (Indiana, PA: Printed by Nupp Printing Co., 1995).

Cooper, Eileen Mountjoy. "Whiskey Run: Where Coal Dust Mixed With Murder," Oral History Feature Category of *Pennsylvania Heritage*, Spring 1980, http://paheritage.wpengine.com/article/whiskey-run-where-coal-dust-mixed-murder/

DellaMea, Chris. *Iselin, PA,* https://www.coalcampusa.com/westpa/indiana/iselin-pennsylvania/iselin-pennsylvania.htm

Ferrandiz, Susan. A dissertation: *McIntyre, Pennsylvania, The Everyday Life Of A Coal Mining Company Town: 1910-1947 (photos, documents, memories of town residents),* 2001, http://204.235.148.201/history_of_mcintyre.htm

Guthrie, Woody. *The Dying Doctor,* https://www.woodyguthrie.org/Lyrics/Dying_Doctor.htm

Harris, James W. "A Picture Essay," *Coal People, Contemporary Images of Northern Appalachia* (Indiana, PA: Printed by Nupp Printing Co., 1995).

Jones, Jr, James B. "Coal Mining in the Cumberland Plateau, 1880-1930," *National Park Services: Appalachian Cultural Resources Workshop Papers* (1880-1930), 2008, https://www.nps.gov/parkhistory/online_books/sero/appalachian/sec9.htm

Katarski, Jeffry. "Communities in Profile-- Iselin, Altman, McIntyre," Pittsburgh, PA: *Tribune-Review,* December 5, 1993.

Kologie, Carl. "Ribbon-Cutting Ceremony For Water Renovation Project" written by the Assistant Editor of the *Indiana Evening Gazette*. (Indiana, PA: *Indiana Evening Gazette*, January 12, 1981).

Lambert, James M. Essay, "The construction of the Rosborough farmhouse" contributed to *WPML Seller Disclosure Statement Attachment A* written by his sister, Marie Lambert McGee; reprinted in Chapter 22, *Iselin,* 2022.

Lambert, James M. Essay, "Will and Ned Gribbon."

Loy, Matt, supplemented by Hengeveld, Matthew R. *The Legend of the Molly Maguires,* The Pennsylvania State University, 2021

McGee, Marie Lambert. “They called him Mr. Jim,” Essay, Chapter 12, *Iselin,* 2022.

McGee, Marie Lambert. *WPML Seller Disclosure Statement Attachment A* written by Marie Lambert McGee, Administrator for the Estate of Sara L. Lambert, her mother.

Mountjoy, Eileen. “Iselin Family*,”* part of the series *Coal Culture: People, Lives, and Stories,* Indiana University of Pennsylvania,1981,

https://www.iup.edu/library/departments/archives/coal/people-lives-stories/iselin-family.html

Mountjoy, Eileen. *The Company Town of Iselin,* Special Collections and Community Archives at Indiana University of Pennsylvania,

https://www.iup.edu/library/departments/archives/coal/mines-and-company-towns/the-company-town-of-iselin.html

Semuskie, Stan. “There was another special thing about Iselin,” Essay, Chapter 15, *Iselin,* 2022.

Travis, Merle. *Sixteen Tons,* https://www.youtube.com/watch?v=5pfVvqLM_e4

Tassin, Susan Hutchison. *Pennsylvania Ghost Towns: Uncovering The Hidden Past* (Mechanicsburg, PA: Stackpole Books, 2007).

Wallace, Anthony F. C. *Patch Towns,* https://amphilsoc.org/exhibits/wallace/patches.htm

Watson, James T., Diodato, Foster D., and Lauch, Milt. "Design and Performance of the Artificial Wetlands Wastewater Treatment Plant at Iselin, Pennsylvania," *Tennessee Valley Authority, Office of Natural Resources and Economic Development*, a government publication. (Chattanooga, Tennessee: July 1986, revised December 1986).

Booklets:

Golden Jubilee of Holy Cross Catholic Church, Iselin, Pennsylvania 1908-1958, a booklet printed by the Church, 1958.

Diamond Jubilee of Holy Cross Church, Iselin, PA 1908-1983, a booklet printed by the Church, 1983.

Related websites:

Church of the Good Shepherd Parish, Kent, PA,

https://www.goodshepherdkent.org/about/Pages/default.aspx

Cook Forest State Park, PA,

https://www.dcnr.pa.gov/StateParks/FindAPark/CookForestStatePark/Pages/default.aspx

"Dr Betty Hayes (1912-1984) and her father, Dr Leo Zeno Hayes (1878-1942)," Mt Zion Historical Society, https://mtzionhistoricalsociety.org/history/stories/the-valleys-coal-miners-doctor/

"Frequency - DJT Electrical Training" https://studylib.net/doc/18177617/frequency---djt-electrical-training

"Horse-Drawn Railways," https://en.wikipedia.org/wiki/List_of_horse-drawn_railway

"How Coal Works," *Union of Concerned Scientists*, last updated December 2017, https://www.ucsusa.org/resources/how-coal-works

"How Green Was My Valley," https://en.wikipedia.org/wiki/How_Green_Was_My_Valley_(film)

Indiana County Municipal Services Authority,

http://icomsa.org/About-Us/ICMSA-About-Us

"Injuries, Illnesses, and Fatalities" written for the US Bureau of Labor Statistics, last modified May 2019,

https://www.bls.gov/iif/oshwc/osh/os/osar0012.htm#:~:text=-Coal%20mining%20is%20a%20relatively,the%20Bureau%20of%20Labor%20Statistics

"It's A Wonderful Life," https://en.wikipedia.org/wiki/It%27s_a_Wonderful_Life

"Operation Scarlift and Mine Reclamation in Pennsylvania," Pennsylvania Department of Environmental Protection,

https://www.dep.pa.gov/Business/Land/Mining/AbandonedMineReclamation/OperationScarlift/Pages/default.aspx

"Pennsylvania has the most abandoned coal mines in the U.S.," *WITF Let's Discover*, https://www.witf.org/2022/02/10/pennsylvania-has-the-most-abandoned-coal-mines-in-the-u-s-how-245-million-will-help/#

"Privies," *Monticello,* monticello.org/research-education/thomas-jefferson-encyclopedia/privies/

"Project Zero," *The Theory of Multiple Intelligences,* http://www.pz.harvard.edu/projects/multiple-intelligences

"Sulfur Dioxide," *Queensland Government*, last reviewed June 2022,

https://www.qld.gov.au/environment/management/monitoring/air/air-pollution/pollutants/sulfur-dioxide

"Sulfur Dioxide and Coal," *Global Energy Monitor*, last edited April 2021,

https://www.gem.wiki/Sulfur_dioxide_and_coal

Photography portfolios

https://stan-semuskie.smugmug.com/Family/Bottleworks-gallery

https://stan-semuskie.smugmug.com/Photo-Restorations/Iselin-Pennsylvania

https://stan-semuskie.smugmug.com/Family/Mrs-Lamberts-105-Birthday-Party/i-ZWwwBSt

Obituaries

Elizabeth Hayes, MD (1912-1984),

https://www.nytimes.com/2022/04/01/obituaries/elizabeth-hayes-overlooked.html

James P. Lambert (1909-1981),

Indiana Evening Gazette April 27, 1981.

Nick Kolavchick (1906-1977),

https://oaklandcemetery.us/profile/nick-kovalchick/

Sara L. Lambert (1909-2016),

https://www.legacy.com/us/obituaries/triblive-valley-news-dispatch/name/sara-lambert-obituary?id=7192946

Index

About the Author

Sara Lambert Bloom, active researcher and author, mentor, and advocate for social justice; retired oboist, teacher, editor, commissioning and recording artist; widow of eminent American oboist Robert Bloom.

RobertandSaraLambertBloom.com

B. 1944 in Indiana County Hospital; raised in Iselin, PA
Valedictorian, Class of 1962, ERHS, Elders Ridge, PA
B. Music, Pi Kappa Lambda, 1966, Oberlin Conservatory
M. Music, 1968, Yale School of Music
Noted oboist and teacher, Marquis *Who's Who* (est. 1898)
Emerge Maine, class of 2009

Pre-Publication review of *Iselin—The Rich History of a Western Pennsylvania Coal Town in Appalachia—The Inspiring Story of Unrelenting Citizen Advocates for Social Justice*

"You should be applauded for capturing the culture and spirit of Iselin, the mining boom, and the visions of your father. You have so eloquently captured an important keepsake of our heritage."

Michael Duffalo, Executive Director of the Indiana County Municipal Services Authority for 46 years, from its inception in 1973 through his retirement in 2019.

Reviews of one of several publications:

The Robert Bloom Collection, a 42-volume set of scores and parts to the editions of 18-century music and compositions of her late husband, the eminent American oboist Robert Bloom (1908-1994), compiled and edited by Sara Lambert Bloom, including her comments and insights in a preface to each volume, self-published 1998.

"Her erudition and burning commitment to this project shine through on every page...her prose often reads like poetry." Daniel Stolper, Editor, The Double Reed

"Your work compares with the Bernstein papers as a most impressive preservation of an American artist's work. Congratulations." James Sinclair, archivist, Charles Ives papers, Yale University

"The service that Mrs. Bloom has rendered to our art, and by extension, to our culture (world wide) is beyond measure." Timothy Eddy, noted American cellist/teacher

Reviews of two of hundreds of live performances:

"Lambert Bloom, with her exquisite sound, displayed peerless quality as a soloist with perfect timing in the exacting scales of the cadenza." *Sarasota Journal*

"A capacity crowd enjoyed the recital featuring the talents of an incredible oboist." *NPR*

Reviews of two CDs released on Centaur:

Sara Lambert Bloom, Premiere Chamber Works, Centaur 2217

"It takes an extraordinary musician to cover such a range, as well as a technically superb instrumentalist." James H. North, *CD NOW* Nov, 1995

"The opening of Harbison's *Concerto for oboe, clarinet and strings*-a substantial work by one of America's best living composers-is unforgettable. Even better is the long-lined, melismatic lyricism of the central *Larghetto* which lingers in the memory as the highest high point." *The American Record Guide*, Sept/Oct 1995

Music From Cranberry Isles, Centaur 2084

"One could easily dismiss this disc as another of those collections of baroque tidbits but that would be fatuous. It is a meeting of like minds and great musicians with a sole purpose: making music and not dissecting it for study.

"Right from the first notes of Telemann's quartets, one gets a sense of something special: an intimacy, a grace and certainly charm that is frequently nowhere to be found in period instrument recordings. Aside from this, Mrs. Bloom, Mr. Baker and their distinguished colleagues play with excellent intonation, fine balance and a commendable sense of ensemble.

"The intimate environs of Isleford's Congregational Church on Little Cranberry Island, Maine work nicely here...I felt I had been invited into the home of friends for an evening of chamber music, much as my ancestor, Robert Carter experienced in Jefferson's music room at Monticello.

“A hands down winner on all counts.”

Michael Carter, *The American Record Guide 1991*

DownEast Magazine reviewing *Music From Cranberry Isles, Centaur 2084*

Mrs Bloom is amused to see the resemblance to every musician on the recording but the oboist, who looks nothing like her but remarkably like her husband. She has made her peace with her relationship with her mentor.

Press Release

AUGUSTA – Governor Janet Mills signed LD 1046 into law on July 19, 2021. Joining her at the ceremonial signing at the State House are the bill's Sponsor, Representative Maureen Terry, D-Gorham and Co-Sponsors Rep. Erin Sheehan, D-Biddeford; Rep. Lori Gramlich, D-OOB; Rep. Tiffany Roberts, D-South Berwick; **along**

with citizen advocates Sara Lambert Bloom, Sandra Ragan, and Maureen White. (Absent from the photo are Co-Sponsors Sen. Donna Bailey, D-York; Rep Margaret Craven, D-Lewiston; Rep Rebecca Millett, D-Cape Elizabeth; Rep. Margaret O'Neil, D-Saco; and Rep. William Pleucker, I-Warren.)

Ceremonial signing of the Hunger Prevention Act, LD1046 Maine State Legislature with Governor Janet T. Mills, July 2021, Sara Lambert Bloom, citizen advocate, far right.